iPad Animation
– how to make stop motion movies on the iPad with GarageBand, iStopMotion and iMovie

Craig Lauridsen

iPad Animation – how to make stop motion movies on the iPad with GarageBand, iStopMotion and iMovie

© 2014 Craig Lauridsen, revised May 2018
Acumen
19 Trevor Terrace, Newtown
Wellington 6021
New Zealand

ISBN 978-0-473-33888-6

The website for this book is *ipadanimation.net*

Go to the website to BUY the ebook (ISBN 978-0-473-33889-3) or other stop motion resources.

Stop Motion

Fast track the learning curve to making your own stop motion movies.
It's fun, it's crazy, it's addictive. iPad Animation leads you through simple and robust processes, helping both beginner and amateur animators make good decisions when creating stop motion on the iPad.

By avoiding the common mistakes, your first movies will have the quality of a more seasoned movie maker. This is a great guide for teachers, parents, children, amateur movie makers and anyone who wants to produce their own stop motion.

By using this book, you'll learn the key competencies across a broad range of learning areas:

- Developing a story and writing it into a **script**
- Recording the **audio** of the script (dialogue, sound effects and music) in GarageBand, and saving it as a soundtrack
- Making **props** and **backgrounds** and creating the **characters** to bring your story to life
- Recording the stop motion **pictures** in iStopMotion
- **Editing** the movie, if required, adding a title and credits in iMovie.

This book is an accessible reference resource; read it cover to cover, or dive into a specific topic and work through the step by step guidelines. While the book covers many universal principles of stop motion, the step by step examples refer to iStopMotion *(www.boinx.com)*, GarageBand and iMovie *(www.apple.com)*.

The Newtown Movie School provides fully interactive stop motion movie making workshops for children. This book is our reference guide and has been published to assist young animators and teachers worldwide.

Craig Lauridsen

Trademarks

Also by Craig Lauridsen:

Creating a Stop Motion Story – Unlock your imagination: A direct step by step instruction for creating story based stop motion on the iPad. Useful as a standalone instruction or as a student summary of the iPad Animation book – *www.ipadanimation.net*

Expanded Story Outlines: Inspiration for improvised story telling in different genres – *www.ipadanimation.net*

Stop Motion Handbook: Creating stop motion on a Mac using iStopMotion, GarageBand and iMovie – *www.stop-motion-handbook.com*

Watch stop motion movies made at **Newtown Movie School** – *www.newtownmovieschool.co.nz*

Downloadable files

There are a number of downloadable music files which accompany the examples in this book. Look for the download instructions in the Projects chapter.

Get the Download files

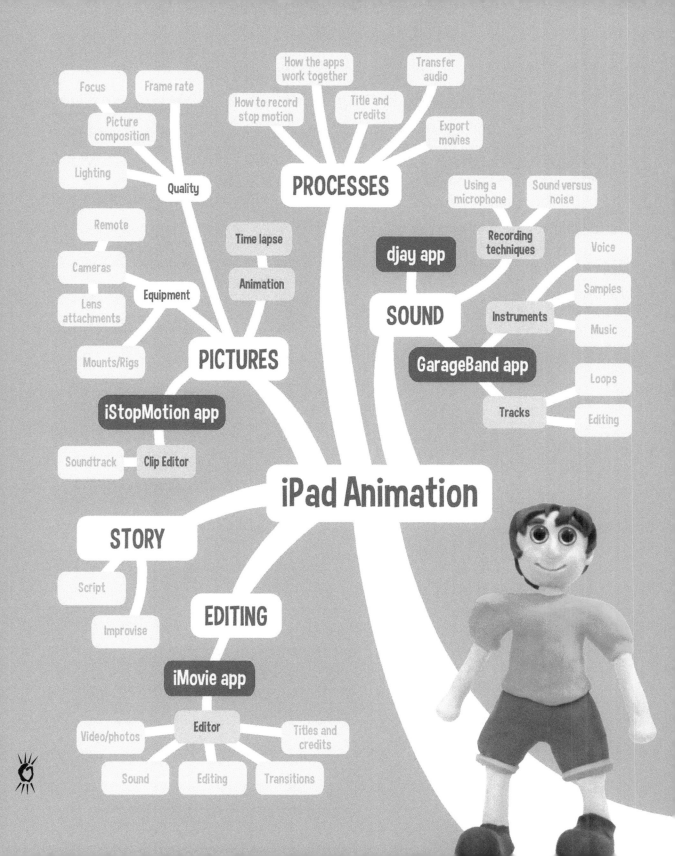

Also by Craig Lauridsen

Available from *www.ipadanimation.net/store.html*

Creating a Stop Motion Story

Unlock your Imagination

A straightforward step-by-step guide to creating a story-driven stop motion movie. Ideal for the classroom and hobby.

Create a complete movie of an original story in a few hours.

3 apps, one iPad, 100% creativity.

An excellent digital media resource for teachers and students.

Story Outlines

Tools for improvising great stories

If you like the story improvisation tool in this book, you'll want to get our book of expanded story outlines customised for various genres such as alien, fairy and spy. Just answer the questions and you'll create awesome original stories.

Story outlines are excellent for developing original story outlines for your movie. Great for improvisation and working in groups.

Genres include: Action, Adventure, Alien, Crime, Desert, Disaster, Documentary, Drama, Epic, Fairy, Fantasy, Gangsta, Ghetto, Horror, Monster, Mystery, Pirate, Romance, Science Fiction, Sports, Spy, Thriller, War, Western and Zombie.

Contents

iPad Animation

The iPad is one of the most exciting recent developments in stop motion movies. Now everyone can participate, and with this book you'll soon be making animation movies like a professional.

Just follow the steps and in a few hours you will have created an original story and a superb stop motion animation, all made 100% on your iPad.

You can make stop motion by yourself or in a group:

One person records the soundtrack and then the pictures

A group records a common soundtrack which is shared to each person to record their own pictures. For a larger project, each person records pictures for one scene

If you want information about resources for stop motion on the iPad go to *www.ipadanimation.net*.

This website also has examples of stop motion movies made on the iPad, so you might want to get inspired before you start. YouTube also has many stop motion movies. Even if they weren't made on an iPad, you'll be able to get ideas about how to improve your movies.

www.ipadanimation.net

Stop motion

Stop motion is a movie made from a sequence of individual pictures. When the pictures are viewed quickly, one after the other, our eyes are 'tricked' into thinking the objects in the pictures are moving.

There are two main types of stop motion – **animation** and **time lapse**.

Animation

A repeating process of:

1) moving the character or object a small amount to dramatise a story or demonstrate a process, and

2) recording a picture

When the pictures match the soundtrack, the character comes alive.

Time lapse

An automatic recording of a sequence of pictures at a certain time interval to produce a faster view of an event. Time lapse compresses time.

1

What makes good stop motion?

There are two broad aspects to making good stop motion movies:

- **The story** – every movie, whether it is a work of fiction or an informative non-fiction topic, needs to have something to say. Your story doesn't have to be original, but you need to tell it well. A story doesn't always need words, but it should show a progression of ideas that benefits the audience.

  'Random' movies, ie actions without any particular story or logic, are popular, but are often an excuse for lazy thinking. It might be fun to make stop motion about a chair moving across the room all by itself, but it is not very creative. Movies are a powerful medium – use them well. Life is too short to make bad movies.

- **Technical quality** – this book covers topics such as image composition, lighting, camera movements, sound and animation effects.

Ask yourself, *"Why should someone watch my movie?"*.

One of the goals of this book is to lead you through proven methods and strategies so even your first stop motion movie is successful.

The apps

This book uses several apps to perform the various tasks for making stop motion movies. And the great thing is, the apps all share the files with each other.

We'll use **GarageBand** for creating a soundtrack, then have a quick look at **djay** from Algoriddim as an alternative for creating a rhythmic soundtrack.

iStopMotion from Boinx is a complete and portable stop motion and time lapse recording studio in one piece of equipment.

We'll edit the stop motion clips into a movie in **iMovie**.

To create stop motion animation on your iPad you'll need these apps:

- **GarageBand** – for the soundtrack,
- **iStopMotion** – for the pictures, and
- **iMovie** – for the titles.

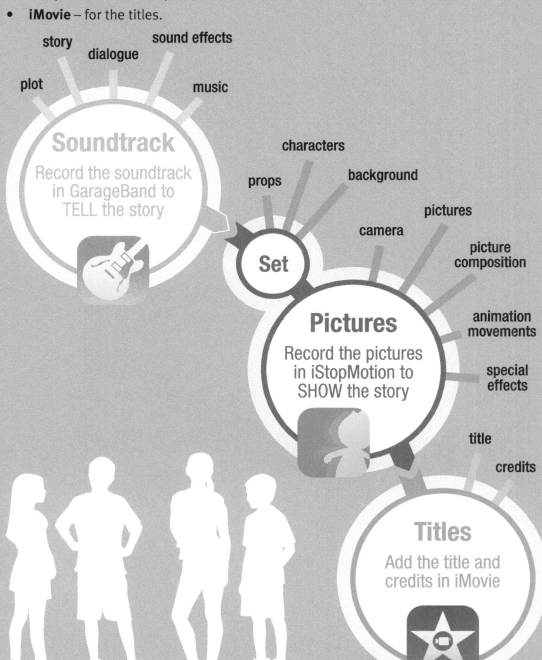

plot · story · dialogue · sound effects · music

Soundtrack
Record the soundtrack in GarageBand to TELL the story

props · characters · background · camera · pictures · picture composition · animation movements · special effects

Set

Pictures
Record the pictures in iStopMotion to SHOW the story

title · credits

Titles
Add the title and credits in iMovie

3

www.iPadAnimation.net

4

5

Process 1
– Starting with the sound

Sound is an important part of a movie experience. It adds emphasis and depth of meaning to the pictures. It is therefore very important the timing of the sounds match the actions in the pictures. It can be hard to watch dialogue that does not match the character movements (lip sync); or where the sound of an effect, such as an explosion, is not coordinated with the pictures. **When you create the soundtrack first, it is easy to achieve perfect alignment between the pictures and the sound.**

Process 1 is suitable for movies which have a story or narrative.

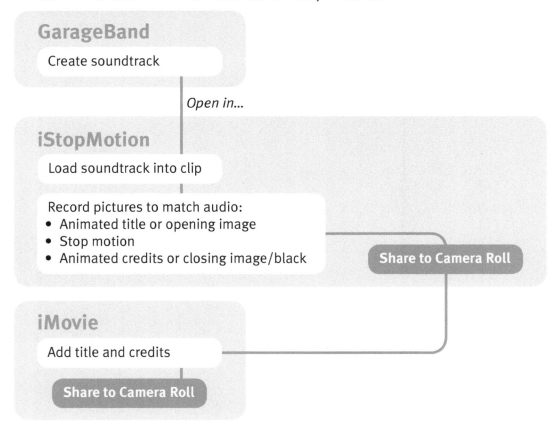

Sound

iStopMotion can have one audio file as the soundtrack. If you don't have a complete soundtrack you will need to record and arrange the dialogue, sound effects and music first – in **GarageBand**.

Pictures

The soundtrack, when imported into iStopMotion, appears in the Timeline and helps you 'see' the sound. One of the keys to successful stop motion is matching the pictures to the sound.

The Timeline below shows that three pictures are required before a dramatic sound.

When there is a dramatic sound, change the camera position to add more emphasis. For example, if the upcoming sound is dialogue show a close up of the character speaking.

Titles and credits

The entire stop motion including title and credits could be animated in **iStopMotion**.

More commonly, the pictures for the title could be recorded as a simple opening image or scene over which the text will be added later in **iMovie**. The length of the title is determined by the soundtrack. Record enough pictures (simple closing image or black) after the last stop motion dialogue/action to reach the end of the soundtrack, otherwise the sound will cut off abruptly at the last picture.

Process 2
– Starting with the pictures

Where stop motion pictures show a process or event in time lapse, you may choose to record the pictures first and then add a soundtrack afterwards. Deciding the length of the movie before you start will help you calculate the number of pictures required, eg 60 seconds x 10 FPS = 600 pictures, 60 seconds x 30 FPS = 1800 pictures.

For story-driven stop motion it is challenging to decide how many pictures to record for each action without the context of the soundtrack as a guide – Process 1 is easier.

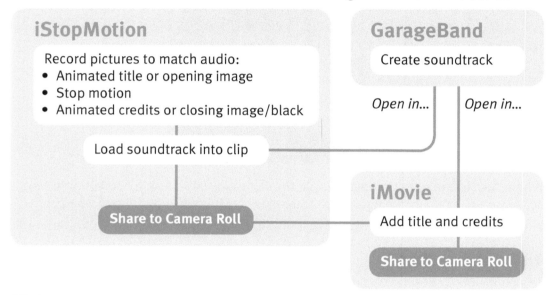

Pictures

Record all stop motion pictures including for those for title and credits in **iStopMotion**. The title could be animated or recorded as a simple opening image or scene over which the text will be added in **iMovie**. The credits can be animated, recorded as a simple closing images or black, or can be added later in **iMovie**.

Sound

Create the soundtrack in **GarageBand** or select an audio file. After all the pictures have been recorded , the soundtrack can be added in **iStopMotion** or **iMovie**. If you add the soundtrack in iStopMotion, make sure you have enough pictures to reach the end of the Soundtrack to avoid the sound being cut short.

Process 3 – Editing a project

This process is suitable for larger projects where there are many picture or sound clips, or a number of people creating content.

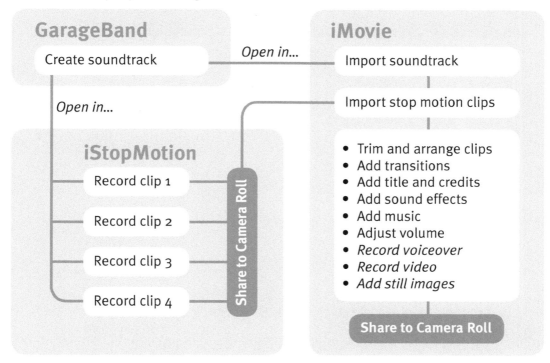

Depending on the nature of the stop motion it is usually easier to create the soundtrack in **GarageBand** first so the project has a defined outline. Alternatively, a storyboard may be useful to outline the project.

Use **iStopMotion** to record clips of stop motion content. Clips can be recorded out of order, by different people on different devices and with different speeds. If the clips need to match a particular part of the soundtrack use the offset feature (see *Audio options* on page 159) to start the right part of the soundtrack for that clip. If possible, record one second of additional pictures at the start and end of each clip to allow flexibility for transitions during editing.

Use **iMovie** to edit the clips, soundtrack and other content into a movie. Match each clip with the full soundtrack to ensure it runs seamlessly across all the clips.

Tips for making great stop motion

- The best movies have a clear story or message. Whether your stop motion is a fiction film, short film, advertisement, documentary or a scientific visual study, is it clear what the movie is about?

- Take care to get the best sound recording you can. It adds far more to the quality of the movie than you'd expect

- Keep it short. If you can tell a five minute story in three minutes, do it!

- Engage your audience early – what is the first thing that is seen and heard in your stop motion?

- Position the camera so the talking character is clearly visible. If you are working with small characters, such as LEGO® or Plasticine®, place the camera down at their eye level

- Arrange the characters and objects at the start of each scene so it is easy for the audience to understand that part of your story

- Everything happens for a purpose. Nothing is random

- Tape everything to the table so it can't move. Use duct tape to secure backgrounds, sets, stands etc.

- If the soundtrack is to be dominant, eg a music video, match the pace of movement in the pictures with the tone of the music

- Keep it simple, and keep it fun

- If the movie is longer than five minutes, include short picture scenes to break the story or flow of information. Choose music which has a strong tune or interesting interlude to emphasise the story break. Choose pictures to convey the tone of the story, eg a wide angle panorama to indicate bigness or loneliness, or try something arty or quirky

- Before you start, get permission from all contributors if you intend to upload the movie to the internet or show if publicly.

Every part of the
story happens
for a purpose

Creating a story, devising a plot

Developing the story and script

The first stage in creating any iPad Animation is to decide what the stop motion is about.

- **A story is the main event that takes place in the movie.** It should fit on one page.

- **A script is the specific detail of what everyone says and does.** It will be many pages depending on the length of the movie.

It is possible to tell a great story really badly, or to tell a boring story brilliantly (the second of these may be more watchable). Aim for a good story told through a good script.

Some people say that in all the world there are only six stories. All other stories are in some way a variation of these core stories. This is why we see a lot of similarities between the stories in different movies, eg in *Lion King* and *Madagascar 2* (and others) a son wants to please his father but instead causes a disaster and runs away. After some soul searching he comes back home to seek restoration and succeeds.

There are many ways to create a story and script for stop motion including writing, adapting and improvising. Here is an overview of the stages of development for three methods:

	Write a script	Adapt a story	Improvise a story
Ideas	✔		✔
Writing	✔		
Editing	✔	✔	
Recording audio	✔	✔	✔

You need to find the core story and omit information that is not important to the story or that can be shown another way. Remember that every second of soundtrack needs to be animated. So if in doubt, make it shorter.

Writing a script

This is a bit like writing an essay, but the result is a movie script. If you want an original movie you'll need to write a script crafted from the idea of a unique story.

Go to *Writing a script* on page 19.

Adapting a story for a script

Written stories can be a good start, but they need to be adapted for a movie.

If you've ever read a book and then watched the movie version you'll know that it might take ten hours to read the book, but only 2 hours to watch the movie. The movie aims to tell the main essence of the story. A lot of the story has either been conveyed in another way, or has been omitted.

Go to *Adapting a story for a script* on page 24.

Improvising a story

A quick, fun and collaborative way to create a story is improvisation. This method is great for group work because everyone gets to take part in creating the soundtrack.

Don't write anything down. Don't try to plan ahead. Just answer the story outline questions one at a time and you'll create an original story.

Go to *Improvising a script* on page 26.

Writing a script

Some stop motion is best with a written script:

- A non-fiction event or process. Work out what needs to be said and what can be shown (see *Water Cycle project* on page 257)
- A longer fiction story (see *My Story project* on page 245)
- Thirty second advertisement. A good exercise in very concise writing of 20 to 50 words in a maximum of 30 seconds (see *TV advertisement* on page 18)
- Comic strip. Working from a common scenario, specified characters and behaviours, each short script tells of a unique event in the life of the character
- Retelling of a popular story or fable – edit a short version which is easy to read and quick to animate.

Here is an overview of the process to write a script for your stop motion movie.

Step 1: Writing a premise

A story needs to be about something. That 'something' is the premise. It's the central idea and the reason people want to watch the movie. It's often an open question: **'What might happen if...?'**

> **Movie premises**
>
> *Bee Movie (2007) – what might happen if bees find out that humans are taking their honey?*
>
> *High School Musical (2006) – what might happen if someone follows their own dreams instead of dreams other people have for them?*
>
> *Monsters Inc. (2001) – what might happen if children stop being scared of monsters?*
>
> *Toy Story 1 (1995) – what might happen if toys come to life when their owner is out of the room?*
>
> *Groundhog Day (1993) – what might happen if you live the same day over and over again and have the chance to change your choices?*

A good premise should be:

- brief – ideally one sentence (maximum 25 words)
- an idea that jumps out at you
- in the present tense.

Sometimes people waste a lot of time trying to improve a story that's not worth telling because the premise is not interesting.

Step 2: Questions which develop the premise

Use techniques like brainstorming or mind maps to get good ideas that develop your premise.

Suppose your premise is 'What might happen if I wake up one morning and find I can fly?'

What questions come to mind?

- Where will I fly to?
- How fast can I fly?
- What can I do that is better than walking?
- In what way is flying more risky than walking?
- How could I use this ability for my own advantage?
- How would I use this ability to benefit others?
- How long will this ability last – just one day, from now on, or until I make a mistake?
- Would I be the same size as I am now, or shrunk to the size of a bird?
- Do I fly with my arms, or have I grown wings?
- Would I still go to school?
- What would my parents think?
- What would my friends think?
- What would be my greatest goal with my ability to fly?
- What would be my greatest barrier to achieving this goal?

Your answers to these questions may lead you to a particular idea which could become your story.

Alternatively, these answers may help you define a character which you can write into an existing story. For example, come up with your own original version of *'The three little (flying) pigs'*.

The next step is to take all those ideas you've come up with and combine the best of them into a story.

Step 3: Writing the story outline

A story outline connects the various separate ideas you want in the story. One good way to develop a story outline is to use small plot cards. On each card write one event, important action or key line of dialogue. Use as many cards as you need to tell the whole story.

Place the cards down on a table in a line and read through the story:

- Does the story flow?
- What happens if you move a card to a different order?
- Do you need to add scenes on extra cards?
- Do each of the main characters have a significant role?

When you are happy with the way your story develops, number each card so they don't get out of order.

Writing the story in three parts

Here is a common format for a dramatic story which is told in three parts (also called 'acts'):

- The **first part** introduces the hero of the story, the problem and also the villain
- The **second part** moves the heroine into the heart of the problem. By the end of the second part they are at a point when all hope seems lost
- The **third and final part** has a final confrontation and resolution of the problem.

If the pace of the story was drawn as a line it would look like this:

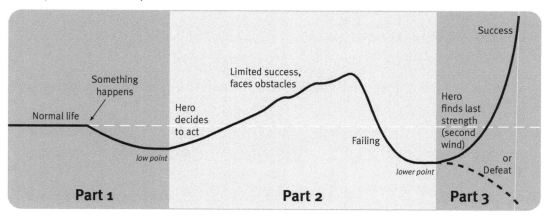

Step 4: Writing the story into a script

Take your story outline and add details to bring the story to life. Determine which characters you need and write the lines of dialogue. List the artwork/props required.

> *Trey Parker and Matt Stone, creators of South Park, share this tip for developing a story outline. If every point in a story outline can be connected to the next point with 'and then', the story seems to have no purpose. Whereas, if every point in the story is connected to the next point with 'but' or 'therefore', you have an engaging story.*

> *Emma Coats, a Pixar story artist, suggests this structure for the outline of a story: "Once upon a time there was ___. Every day, ___. One day ___. Because of that, ___. Because of that, ___. Until finally ___."*

Make notes about actions and scene changes – you don't want a movie that is non-stop talking without a break.

It can be easier to record dramatic or 'acted' voices if people don't need to concentrate on reading. A script can be written as a sequence of points so the actual words are improvised when recorded.

Make the opening interesting or exciting to catch the audience's attention.

Leave spaces in the script for characters and the audience to ponder the seriousness of the situation, and to increase the tension, before the hero makes a move.

Read through the script. Is the story clear and does it have the right pace?

Make some connection between the start and the end, eg an overlooked object or idea from the start becomes useful in the resolution of the problem.

Labelling the scenes (optional)

If your story is longer, or will be animated by several groups, add labels to your script. Scene labels might indicate the location or time of day and could be used as a guide to change the camera position or background. Labels in a movie script are different to chapter headings in a book because they describe the location rather than the action. It is conventional to use capital letters.

When your story is written, go to *Recording voice* on page 37.

For more information on creating strong stories and developing compelling scripts, refer to these resources:

* *Screenplay: The foundations of screenwriting* by Syd Field
* *Story: Substance, structure, style and the principles of screenwriting* by Robert McKee
* International Central Institute for Youth and Educational Television (IZI) *www.izi.de.*

Writing a TV advertisement

A fun stop motion project is to create a television advertisement. The script needs a very clear, persuasive message – which could actually be a very, very short story.

Step 1: Write down the product or service you want to advertise

Step 2: Name three FEATURES

List three features or good points (facts) about the product or service, eg the wrapper is edible, the battery lasts for a month, it fits in your pocket.

Step 3: Name three BENEFITS to the customer, public or audience

For each feature write HOW the customer will benefit. The customer needs to be convinced that your product or service will save them money, be more convenient, be safer, smell better etc. The benefits can be funny or serious, but must be possible or believable.

Step 4: Write the advertisement

Using the benefits, write the script for a 30 second advertisement. If you are advertising a relaxing holiday you'll want to have a relaxed pace, so might only have time for 20 – 30 words. If it is a new 'must have, get in quick' thing, you'll probably talk faster and fit in 50 words.

Time yourself as you read the advertisement – 30 seconds is 30 seconds – not 32. Are there any wasted words you can remove?

Read your script to someone else. Do they feel you've convinced them to buy? Change what you've written if you need to.

Step 5: Make your stop motion advertisement

When you are ready to record your advertisement, go to *Recording voice* on page 37.

Advertisements don't require a title or credits. It can be fun to combine several different advertisements together so they can be viewed as a 'commercial break' like on TV.

Adapting a story for a script

Some written work, such as short poems or prose may already be suitable for a soundtrack and should not require adapting.

However, for most written stories **the biggest task is to reduce the amount of words** to achieve a shorter script. For example, it may take ten hours to read the book whereas the big screen movie is only 90 minutes long. The script needs to tell the main essence of the story in the style of the chosen genre (see *Genre* on page 25).

Here are some examples:

Written story	Adapted for stop motion
It was a dark and scary night. The wind rustled through the trees and gave a shiver to your bones. Somewhere around midnight, the faint cry of a distant wolf pierced the darkness. Suddenly there was a crash at the door. The sound echoed around the metal hut like a ricocheting bullet.	**Sound:** Wind sounds with distant wolf howl (3 seconds). Loud sound of crash on metal with echo (2 seconds). **Background:** Dark, indistinct shapes with vertical strokes representing tree trunks. A full moon casts a ghostly reflection across part of the background. On one side is a cut away view of a small metal hut. **Animation:** Show the whole background for 3 seconds. When the crashing sound starts, show a close up of the hut followed by a rapid sequence of parts of the hut.
I'd been waiting at the bus stop for almost an hour and not even one vehicle had passed. It was the hottest day of summer and I was melting. I tried to think 'cool' thoughts like ice cream and soda, but that was just torture. Then an elephant turned up. "Hop on", it said.	**Sound:** Nature sounds such as crickets, or annoying 'elevator' type music (7 seconds, then a voice says "Hop on". **Background:** Street scene with bus stop. **Animation:** Show empty street. Character paces up and down street (3 seconds), looks at watch (close up for 1 second), character slumps to sit on ground (2 seconds). Large shadow moves over character (1 second). Character looks up and against the sun sees silhouette of elephant (2 seconds).

Characters need something to say unless you want a narrator to do all the talking.

Written story	Adapted for stop motion
Eva and Simon had never been to Mars before. They'd seen pictures of it, of course, but to actually be there was almost beyond words. "It's so beautiful", cried Eva.	**Narrator:** Eva and Simon had never been to Mars before. **Simon:** I'm speechless! **Eva:** It's so ... beautiful.
Quick pass me the guitar and I'll play you a song.	**Zebo:** Quick, pass me the guitar *(starts playing)*.

When you are ready to record your adapted story, go to *Recording voice* on page 37.

Improvising a script

Sometimes the best way to record dramatic voices is to improvise the story as you record (no script!).

The story is uniquely creative, there is nothing to memorise, so all effort can be put into voice tone (see *My Story project* on page 245).

To start off, decide the location, event or time when the story begins. It could be a fictitious place or an historical event. Then just answer the questions one at a time into a microphone and you'll create an original story.

Here are some questions you can use to create a story:

1) Where are you? (*or* What do you feel? What you do see? What are you doing?)
2) What happens?
3) What do you do about it?
4) What stops you?
5) What is the worst outcome?
6) What is the last chance for success?
7) What is the final outcome?

Download a printable copy of this story outline from *www.ipadanimation.net/store.html*.

These seven questions prompt the answers to create the story. Don't try to plan ahead. Don't write anything down. **One question at a time, decide the right voice tone for that part of the story and record the dialogue as it is improvised.**

For the shortest stop motion, answer each question with one short sentence. You may end up with a movie that is around one minute long. Or for a longer soundtrack, use each question as a prompt to develop that part of the story.

If working with a group, it is not necessary to audition 'parts' as each person will answer their question from the perspective they feel makes sense. Several people can share the voice of one character.

We've also developed longer story outlines (which have more questions) for different types of story genres such as alien, fairy and gangster. For more information go to *www.ipadanimation. net/store.html*.

When you are ready to record your improvised story, go to *Recording voice* on page 37.

21

Part 1

Opening scene – Where are you? What do you feel? What do you see? What are you doing?
Defines the movie's time, place, theme and tone

Cause incident – What happens?
The event that sets the plot in motion

First turning point – What do you do about it?
The event that sets the hero on their journey

Part 2

Confrontation and conflict – What stops you?
The heroine forges ahead on the mission but faces obstacles

Defeat – What is the worst outcome?
The point at which all hope seems lost

Part 3

Second turning point – What is your last chance for success?
The life or death event that will test the hero's strength, resolve and moral courage

Resolution – What is the final outcome?
The payoff in which the heroine either triumphs or sacrifices themselves for the greater good

Tips to develop a story

Watch and learn

You can learn how to write a good story by watching other people's movies – both good and bad. Watch all sorts of movies, not just stop motion ones, and not just your favourite type either.

The story must have a point

The story has to be about something or it will not capture the audience. A common plot is about someone whose life has been interrupted by an event or threat of an event. The story is about how they try to sort it out.

Every part of the story should happen for a purpose so it is easy to understand what is happening – nothing is random.

Movies are more successful if they have a good story rather than great special effects.

Even if your movie is mostly about a battle, take the time to develop a story to explain the battle or action sequence:

- What is at stake?
- Who is on each side, and why?
- What happens if the battle is won?
- What happens if the battle is lost?

Choose a hero

Movies should have a hero/ine (also called a protagonist). The hero can be one person, a group of people, an object or a place. They do not always have to be nice, but they should be intriguing.

Make your hero/ine likeable and make their dilemmas something everyone can relate to. Many stories have a hero that the audience would like to be friends with.

Structure your story

Every story needs several parts – a beginning, a middle and an end.

When you have more confidence you can mix them up – start your story in the middle and follow it with the end. Then finish by telling the start of the story. For example, if you start your story with the ending, eg the villain knocks at the door, then tell rest of the story from the beginning so that we can see how the events led up to the villain knocking at the door.

Longer movies often have small side stories to help lead towards the one big story.

Avoid being linear

A story that starts at the very beginning and progresses through each event systematically may not be very exciting.

Don't tell the audience everything at once. Make your audience wonder what's going to happen next. But if you are going to reveal a mystery, make sure the outcome is worth waiting for.

Think about the ending first

In the movie *Titanic*, the director James Cameron ended the movie with an elderly lady who had been on the Titanic being reunited with a necklace she lost when the boat sank. He wrote the story about the Titanic from the point of view of that lady – starting when she was a young girl, the special occasion when she received the necklace and why she was on the boat.

Include a twist

The bigger the twist, the more the audience must feel they should have seen it coming. You need to plant ideas in the minds of your audience. You don't want to give the end away but the viewer should feel that the twist was, on reflection, inevitable and believable.

In *Madagascar – Escape 2 Africa*, a cranky old lady chases the lion at the start of the movie. She appears again chasing some penguins. When the movie is at its climax the old lady becomes the solution to the problem – to chase off the villain. The end is a surprise but also totally logical.

Don't try to be too clever

Simple stories work best. Don't try to be too clever or complex.

Good stories often include true events from the writer's life. For example, if you love animals, you may be able to write a good story about someone who makes friends with wild animals or even dinosaurs.

Be original

Be true to yourself. Don't simply copy others. You may be tempted to use famous quotes or jokes from other people's movies – this might be OK when you are learning to make movies but try to come up with your own funny lines. Good movies stand out because they are unique.

Humour

Look out for little moments which give the audience a smile. You don't need to turn every movie into a comedy, but when recording the audio you may want to keep a word slip up or ad lib. Look out for areas where the choice of props can add interest, or a character movement can add personality. It could simply be pausing between action and response allowing the audience time to ponder what is going to happen.

Pixar's Rules of Storytelling

Emma Coats, *Pixar* story artist, has produced *Pixar's 22 Rules of Storytelling*. See the full list on *www.aerogrammestudio.com/2013/03/07/pixars-22-rules-of-storytelling*. Here are some of them:

- Simplify. Focus. Combine characters. Hop over detours. You'll feel like you're losing valuable stuff but it sets you free

- What is your character good at, comfortable with? Throw the opposite at them. Challenge them. How do they deal with it?

- When you're stuck, make a list of what wouldn't happen next. Lots of times the material to get you unstuck will show up

- Discount the 1st thing that comes to mind. And the 2nd, 3rd, 4th, 5th – get the obvious out of the way. Surprise yourself

- If you were your character, in this situation, how would you feel? Honesty lends credibility to unbelievable situations

- Coincidences to get characters into trouble are great; coincidences to get them out of it are cheating.

Different types of stories – genre

The genre is the general style of how the story is told. Every story fits into one genre or another, or sometimes they are a combination of several genres. Familiarise yourself with the 'rules' for your genre.

The same story told in the style of different genres will result in completely different movies, even though the characters and events in the story are the same.

Here are some of the basic rules for popular genres (search *'movie genre'* for more information):

- **Action** – high energy movies, stunts, chases, rescues, battles. Often two dimensional – good guy/bad guy. Includes movies about an outlaw fighting for justice or battling a tyrant (*Robin Hood, Zorro* or *Star Wars*), pirates (*Pirates of the Caribbean, Hook*) or searching for a lost city or for hidden treasure (*Indiana Jones*)

- **Comedy** – light hearted plots deliberately designed to amuse and provoke laughter by exaggerating every aspect of the story. Includes movies such as *Zoolander, Monsters Inc., Home Alone* and *The Princess Bride*

25

- **Drama** – serious life stories with realistic situations and characters. Not focused on special effects, comedy or action. Includes movies such as *Miss Potter, Saving Mr Banks* and *Finding Neverland*

- **Horror** – includes a hero who has a flaw and a fear. Your 'monster' needs to be truly frightening, and you need to include several 'false alarms' to increase tension. You also need to isolate your hero so that they have no escape from the monster. At the end, suggest that the monster is not really gone. Horror movies include the stop motion *Coraline*

- **Romance** – story revolves around the romantic involvement of the hero/ine who needs to make decisions based on a newly-found romantic attraction. The appeal of these movies is in the dramatic reality of the emotions expressed by the characters. The story needs a happy ending (or at least bittersweet). Movies include *Titanic, Pride and Prejudice* and *High School Musical*

- **Spy** – when a villain tries to obtain secret information, a spy is assigned to stop them. Spy movies often feature secret headquarters, an agent known by a number and an attractive foreign agent who becomes the love of the hero/ine. Popular in movies like *Spy Kids, Johnny English, Cats & Dogs, James Bond* and *Austin Powers.*

There are possibly hundreds of genres and popular trends often create new ones. Here are some more: Adventure, Alien, Animal, Animation, Chick Flick, Crime, Disaster, Documentary, Epic, Family, Fantasy, Film-noir, Mockumentary, Musical, Mystery, Science Fiction, Sequel, Silent, Sport, Thriller, War, Western.

Transform clips into a cinematic experience with sound

Creating a soundtrack using GarageBand

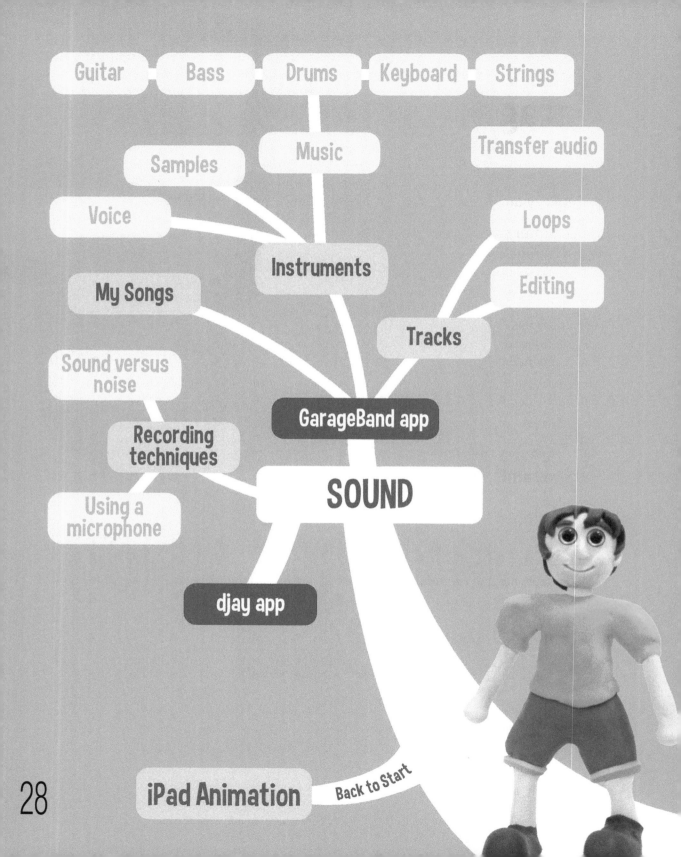

Creating a soundtrack using GarageBand

Adding sound to a stop motion clip can transform it into a cinematic experience. So it is very important to create a soundtrack which matches the energy and mood of the story that will be told in the pictures.

This chapter shows you how to create different types of soundtracks using GarageBand on the iPad.

About copyright

Using music from your favourite band can make your movie really great. However, technically this is stealing. So, while it is a good way to learn how to make movies, you won't be able to have them shown on TV or enter them into a movie competition unless you have obtained permission to use the music. Sometimes it is worth asking the band because they might just say 'yes'!

However, it is usually easier, and quicker, to buy music which includes permission for use in movies for a small cost (see *Getting sound effects and music* on page 34 for information on 'royalty-free' music), or else make your own in GarageBand.

GarageBand

GarageBand is a very powerful audio recording studio which allows you to create high quality soundtracks. It has a very simple interface so anyone can create a soundtrack regardless of their musical level.

To get the full potential from GarageBand, you probably need some musical knowledge but there are many easy features and smart automatic controls to start with.

Regardless of whether your soundtrack is music, sound effects, narration or singing, in GarageBand the files are called 'songs'.

Garageband uses sounds from a wide range of sources such as:

- Voice and speech recorded with a microphone
- Other music and sound effects recorded with a microphone
- Music played with GarageBand's built-in instruments – drums, guitar, bass, keyboards and strings
- Loops
- iTunes music and MP3
- Samples

29

- Actual music recorded from a real instrument such as a keyboard with the USB Camera Adapter

- Actual music recorded from a real guitar using Apogee JAM.

The focus of this chapter is creating soundtracks for stop motion movies. However, audio requirements are diverse, so **this chapter will be useful as an instruction for any project requiring sound.**

We will look at creating soundtracks using:

- **Microphone** – voice and narration. This is the most common method for soundtracks based on telling a story. This example also uses loops and existing music

- **Samples** – making your own groove

- **Music** – using GarageBand's built-in instruments to create a musical song.

GarageBand has four main screens:

- **My Songs** – all the songs made in GarageBand are stored in 'My Songs'. From this screen you can edit an existing song, create a new song and export a song for use in other apps

- **Instruments** – choose the type of sound to record (microphone, drum, guitar, bass, keyboard, strings etc)

- **Recording** – set the controls for the instrument and record the sound into a track

- **Tracks** – edit the various recorded sounds and arrange them into a song or soundtrack. Each song can have up to 32 tracks, ie 32 sounds playing at the same time, depending on the specification of your iPad.

Open GarageBand. If it doesn't open to My Songs, tap the My Songs button in the top left.

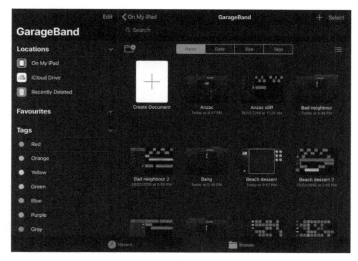

My Songs

Each recorded song has a representative picture with a name, designated *'My Song X'* (until you rename it) and the date the song was last saved. It is a good habit to rename songs to avoid confusion. Tap the song name and use the keyboard to type your unique name.

To start a new song:

- Tap the New Song button at the top or the Create Document button

- Swipe one finger left or right through the instruments until you come to the Audio Recorder.

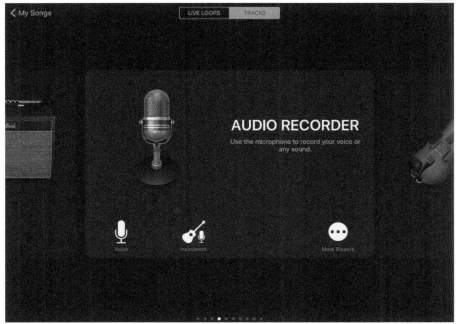

We will use the Audio Recorder to record dialogue with the iPad microphone

- Tap Voice.

Control bar

The control bar appears across the top of most screens. From the left:

- Back to 'My Songs'

- The Instrument Browser button lets you choose a new instrument

- The instrument button displays the instrument screen for the selected track. In this case, the microphone icon indicates the current instrument is the Audio Recorder

- When an instrument screen is displayed, the Tracks button will show an overall view of the whole song

- The Track Controls button for volume and effects

- The FX button shows or hides the FX controls

- Undo. Hold for Redo

- The transport controls move the playhead back to the start of the song or play/ stop the song. The red dot is the Record button

- The master playback volume slider can also be controlled by the iPad volume buttons

- The Metronome button starts and stops the metronome *(it turns blue when on)*

- On the right of the control bar are the Loop Browser for adding loops and music and Song Settings for editing the song

- The playhead (downward pointing marker) moves along the Timeline showing which part of the song is being played. It also marks the point where a new recorded clip will be added. The numbers indicate the timing of the song and are called bars.

The actual length of the song is determined by the tempo and the time signature. These can be changed in Song Settings. GarageBand starts with a tempo of 110 beats per minute and 4/4 time signature, which equates to about 28 bars per minute. The maximum song length is 320 bars (around 11 minutes).

Sections

At the far right of the Timeline is a plus sign button to access a feature called 'Sections'.

Sections are used to create and organise parts of a musical song such as intro, verse, chorus etc. You might use one section for a verse, another for a chorus, and another for the bridge.

A story does not follow this type of pattern, so change the sections to 'Automatic' and your recording can be up to 11 minutes long:

- Tap the Sections button

- Tap Section A

- Set Automatic to 'on'.

Getting sound effects and music

To create a rich, powerful and unique soundtrack you'll need to use the right sound effects and music.

In addition to the music loops and sound effects installed with GarageBand there are many more that can be downloaded for free. Tap Loops, then tap Go to Sound Library.

If you still can't find what you're looking for search for *'royalty free sound effects'* or *'free sound effects'*. Your local library may also have royalty free sound effects on CD.

- Some sites give away **free** files as a sampler to entice you to buy sounds. Other sites simply have free sounds to download. The quality of these sounds can range from excellent to very poor

- **Royalty free** means that once you have paid the appropriate fee, the sound effect or music is yours to use as you wish as often as you like with no further payment

- **Creative Commons** means an artist has chosen to make their work available to others as long as the terms are followed. Read the agreement before using the sound effect or music, eg you may need to give the artist credit.

Go to *www.stop-motion-handbook.com/pages/audio_resources.html* for links to excellent sites for sound effects and music, such as:

- **Blastwave FX** has packs of themed sound effects including *Heroes and Villains*. If you're looking for one resource for action type sound effects this could be it. 1000 sound effects including weapons, impacts, crashes, explosions, vehicles, robots, super powers, ambiences and many more!

    If you're still undecided, check out their free download of sample sounds *(www.blastwavefx.com)*

- **Audioblocks** has sound effects, music and loops. This is a subscription-based site with an introductory offer of 7 days free then a low cost annual fee for unlimited downloads *(www.audioblocks.com)*
- **Pro Sound Effects** specialise in sound effects. They offer individual sounds from $5, monthly plans and themed libraries of sounds *(www.prosoundeffects.com)*
- **Soundsnap** offers credit packs so you can choose the combination of sound effects you want *(www.soundsnap.com)*
- **Instant Sound FX** has a mega bundle of thousands of sounds in a single low cost purchase *(www.instantsoundfx.com)*
- **Audio Hero** provides searchable access to many different sound libraries *(www.audiohero.com)*
- **Sound Bible** offers free sound effects and royalty free sound effects licensed under Creative Commons *(www.soundbible.com)*
- **Freesound** is a collaborative database of free sounds licensed under Creative Commons *(www.freesound.org)*
- **Audio Micro** has free and royalty free sound effects *(www.audiomicro.com)*
- **Free SFX** offers a free download of sound effects *(www.free-sfx.com)*
- **Find Sounds** searches the internet for free sounds of various quality *(www.findsounds.com)*
- **Flash Kit** offers shareware and freeware sounds *(www.flashkit.com/soundfx)*.

Music

Music creates identity for your stop motion. Right from the start of your movie it can set the tone of the story, so take care to choose the right type of music.

The best music for stop motion will probably be instrumental. Don't use popular music from the radio or YouTube because the words make it hard to fit in with your dialogue. Also, you'll need to permission to use it.

Get extra music by searching for *'royalty free music'* or *'free music for video'*. Your local library may have royalty free music on CD.

Here are some excellent sites for free and royalty free music:

- **Freeplay Music** has 15,000 songs that can be used in the classroom and for personal use on YouTube *(www.freeplaymusic.com)*
- **Free Stock Music** – sign up for a free account to download free music. These are high quality tunes provided as an introduction to Audioblocks.com so there are a few pop up windows to navigate *(www.freestockmusic.com)*

- **Audioblocks** has music, loops and sound effects. It is a subscription-based site with introductory offer of 7 days free then a low cost annual fee for unlimited downloads *(www.audioblocks.com)*
- **Purple Planet** has royalty free and free music *(www.purple-planet.com)*
- **Free Music Archive** is a forum for artists to upload free music for others to use *(www.freemusicarchive.org)*
- **MusOpen** is a non-profit site focussed on access to music with free resources. It has classical and royalty free music licensed under Creative Commons *(www.musopen.org)*
- **Audiojungle** has royalty free music. Sign up for the free file of the month *(www.audiojungle.net)*
- **Dig CC Mixter** has music licensed under Creative Commons *(http://dig.ccMixter.org)*.

There are many other sites which have music files including:

- *www.music-for-video.com*
- *www.neumannfilms.net*
- *www.ibaudio.com*
- *www.dawnmusic.com*
- *www.incompetech.com.*

Getting to know GarageBand

GarageBand may be one of the least understood and under-used apps on your iPad.

In this chapter we demonstrate why GarageBand is the best 'go to' app for creating soundtracks.

Recording voices may be one of the most common tasks in GarageBand when creating stop motion soundtracks for a story. Every line of dialogue needs to be recorded.

We'll show you how to get the best quality recording – both technically and dramatically.

Using a microphone

To record a song using the microphone:

- From the My Songs screen tap the New Song button (+) at the top or the Create Document button

$+$

- Swipe one finger left or right through the instruments until you come to the Audio Recorder.

We'll use the Audio Recorder to record dialogue

- Tap Voice.

37

The flickering line on the left indicates how loud the sound is.

Where is the iPad microphone?

The microphone is a small slot on the edge of the iPad. On most iPad devices it is near the front camera – at the opposite end to the Home button. On some recent models, the microphone is a small hole next to the rear camera.

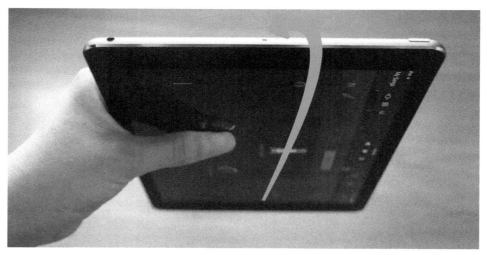

The iPad microphone does an adequate job of recording sound. However, if you want a better quality recording, use a specialised microphone such as Apogee MiC (refer to *www.apogeedigital.com/products/mic*).

Whatever your recording device – iPad or an external microphone – we'll call it the 'microphone'.

Recording level

Talk into the microphone and watch the line. **For the best recording, the green line should be as high as possible.** If the sound is momentarily too loud the top of the line becomes orange. This is not a problem, although the recorded clip may be distorted if the top of the line stays orange for a long time or it becomes red.

If the **average sound level** is a short green line the recorded clip may be too quiet. Make the sound louder or move closer to the microphone.

If the **average sound level** is red at the top of the line the recorded clip will be too loud and distorted. Make the sound quieter or move away from the microphone.

To get the best recording, it is often easier to have a helper operate the iPad and ask them to use hand signals to indicate whether you need to speak more loudly or quietly. This allows you to concentrate on your words and expression.

Position the microphone around 30cm from the source of the sound for a good recording level. You can hold the iPad or use a stand. Just make sure you don't add handling noise into the recording.

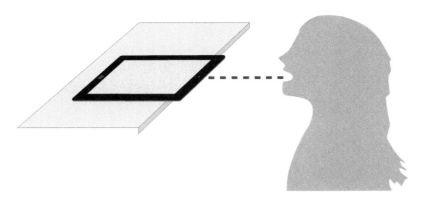

To record sound with more bass, such as a guitar, hang the microphone over the side of a vertical surface, such as a bench. The vertical surface helps to collect more bass sounds.

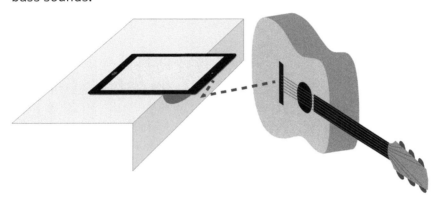

Sound versus noise

Sound has a surprising effect on the quality of a movie. Clear and crisp sound can make bad pictures look better than they are, whereas noisy and muffled sound will make amazing pictures 'feel' second rate.

Professional music and loops are recorded in a studio and are very clear and vibrant. Without a studio, we can still make the best effort to record high quality.

Everywhere you go, there is a combination of **'sound'** – the audio you want to hear – and **'noise'** – the audio you don't want to hear. When you are recording with a microphone, you need to record sound with the least amount of noise:

* Take time to find the quietest space you can

* Listen to determine if the room has any echo, and if so, add soft furnishings such as shutting the curtains, cushions or blankets over hard surfaces

* Listen for background noises such as the drone of a computer, the tick of a wall clock and turn them off or take them out of the room. Think about potential noises – switch off your phone and take off that bracelet or rustling jacket

- Shut the doors and windows to block any noise from outside
- Wait for the plane to fly overhead or for the lawnmower next door to finish.

Larger than life

People recording dialogue are 'voice actors' – they act with their voice.

Reading from a script can sound dull and uninteresting. **Dramatic voices captivate the audience.** If the character is saying they are scared, their voice should sound scared. If they are saying something positive, they should sound happy, and so on. Don'tffshout, but put expression into your voice.

It can be easier to start with just an outline of the key story points and **prompt people to say their lines in their own words and with expression.** Dramatic stories often require a different expression for every line. If the first take is not dramatic enough, immediately record another take, and another, until you are satisfied.

Stand up when recording, as it is easier to breathe deeply and 'throw' your voice.

Clarity

The most common problem with recording dialogue is people speaking too many words too quickly – slow down.

In acted movies we see the actor's mouth movements which help us to determine their words even if they are muffled or slurred. **Stop motion characters often have set mouth shapes so the clarity of the words needs to come from the audio.**

Take care with pronunciation. Make sure you open your mouth wide when talking. Don't take your personality out of your voice, but listen carefully for words that run together or where the diction is not clear. In particular, **make sure the sounds of consonants are crisp** (I call this 'crunchy consonants'), **and have a breath between sentences.** What a shame if your audience can't enjoy your movie because they have no idea what is said! For example, what could this mean?

> "Is the presen forme? Yitza bike".

- Which words need to be pronounced more clearly?
- What actions will be animated, and what timing will they require?

Here is better example of the same words (emphasis in bold):

> "Is this PresenT for ME?" (character looks at package)
> (allow 2 seconds to open package)
> "YEAH! (breath) IT's a BIKE!"

41

Here are some tips to get the best recording of dialogue:

- Take off a rustling jacket or bangles
- Stand tall with both feet firmly on the floor
- Move your arms if it helps to get a more dramatic tone in your voice. You may want to hold something so you're not tempted to fidget
- Take a big breath to fill your lungs with air before your start
- Open your mouth wide and pronounce each word clearly
- Put expression into your voice, but don't shout
- Speak one simple sentence at a time
- Pause between key points in the sentence
- If you are working in a group, have the voice actor stand with their back to the group so they won't get distracted.

Record voices individually

The easiest way to record dialogue is to use one track. This example has all dialogue recorded in one track:

For larger projects it may be necessary to record characters into their own track. This example has three voices recorded into three tracks:

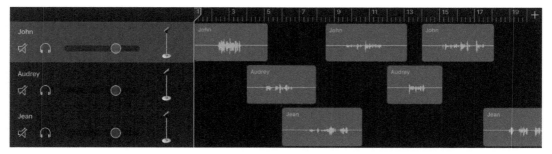

Recording each voice individually allows you to get the best from each person and therefore the best overall recording. It is easy to adjust the timing between each dialogue clip. The volume can be changed for each track or an effect applied to a track.

As an option, each clip can instead be given a name that presents the words that are spoken. For short recording projects undertaken by one person this is probably not necessary, although for larger projects, particularly undertaken by a group, naming at least some clips may help with team communication.

Double tap on a clip and select Rename from the list of editing options. You can also tap and then tap again on the track header to change the track icon picture, if that helps you understand how clips relate to the whole soundtrack.

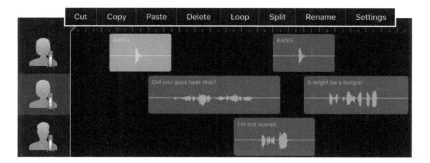

Record all voices together

If you are working with people who have good voice projection, who are familiar with their 'script' and are all likely to give their best performance at the same time, have everyone stand around the microphone and record their voices together.

This might be the quickest method to record, but it can be hard to make changes. Test the recording to make sure each person can be heard. Ask people to move closer or further away from the microphone so each person has a similar volume.

Recording with a microphone

Every time you record with the microphone there are three settings to change:

1) Tap the **Metronome** button in the top right to turn it OFF – *it should not be blue.*

The metronome is useful with built-in instruments and when using headphones. Most stories need dramatic pace not an even beat.

2) Next, tap the Song Settings button in the top right.

Turn OFF the **Count in**.

Settings

Count-In

Metronome Sound   Woodblock >

A count in is good to help the 'band' play their instruments all together. Story dialogue needs to start with silence.

Tap the middle of the screen to close this panel.

3) Lastly, tap the **Sections** button (plus sign) in the top right.

Tap on the number next to Section A (usually '8 bars') and turn ON Automatic section length.

< Song Sections **Section Length**

Automatic

Turn Automatic off, then tap the arrows to change the length of the song section in single-digit increments, or swipe vertically to change by larger values.

Sections are used to create parts of a musical song such as intro, verse, chorus etc. A story does not follow this type of pattern.

Tap the middle of the screen to close this panel.

44

When you are ready to record:

- Find the quietest space you can (see *Sound versus noise* on page 40)

- Position the microphone near the sound source

- Tap Go to Beginning button to make sure the playhead is at the start

- Follow the sound recording process on the next page.

It is often easier to record several takes one after the other in the same clip. Try experimenting with different voice expressions. Remember to pause and leave 2 seconds of silence between them.

It is important that the last word is spoken confidently before reaching for the stop button – there is no need to rush.

If you make a mistake with your words, record the dialogue again as a second take. When you edit the soundtrack later you'll be able to delete the parts you don't want and, if necessary, reorder them into the right order (see *Editing tracks* on page 92).

GarageBand tracks

After you've made a recording, tap the Tracks button in the top left.

For a closer look at the clip, use the **pinch** gesture – *touch two fingers on the screen and spread them apart to zoom in, or bring them closer together to zoom out.*

Sound recording process

Recording high quality sound is an important part of a stop motion movie. Follow this process to record dialogue or sound effects with the microphone:

- Say *"Quiet on set"* so everyone in the room knows to be quiet

- Tap the red Record button

- Wait two seconds to record silence at the start
  – this will make it easier to edit later

- **Speak clearly and expressively,** or make the sound

- Wait two seconds to record silence at the end

- If you think you can improve
  (make your words clearer or put more expression into your voice), keep recording and have another go, otherwise

- Tap Stop – and everyone can relax.

If your sound is crisp and clear your audience will think the pictures are better than they are.

If your sound is poor, even the best pictures in the world won't stop your audience thinking the movie is low quality.

Your recorded clip may look something like this:

A thin line indicates silence | The recorded dialogue should have a solid shape

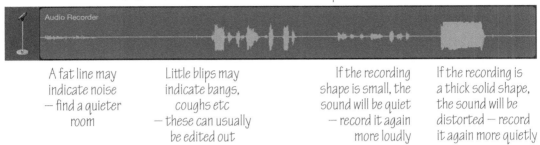

A fat line may indicate noise — find a quieter room | Little blips may indicate bangs, coughs etc — these can usually be edited out | If the recording shape is small, the sound will be quiet — record it again more loudly | If the recording is a thick solid shape, the sound will be distorted — record it again more quietly

Tap the Play button and listen to the recording:

- Are the words clear (diction and pronunciation)?
- Is it expressive enough (tone and volume)?
- Are there unwanted noises or distractions?

If you're not happy with the recording, record it again. Don't try to delete a bad recording at this stage as we'll do editing later. Otherwise, move on to record the next part of the story.

If you are confident that you have made a good recording there is no need to go to the Tracks screen after each recording.

Recording additional dialogue

For quick handling it can be easier to **record all dialogue clips in one track** as it saves a number of steps and avoid potential mistakes. We'll spread the recorded clips across multiple tracks later.

Simply make sure the playhead is AFTER the end of the last recorded clip and you're ready.

To move the playhead, simply tap the new position on the Timeline. Avoid dragging the playhead as you may unintentionally move clips.

Tap the Microphone button to return to the recording screen and you're ready to record the next clip.

47

Recording additional dialogue in different tracks

For longer soundtracks or projects, you may want to record each person directly into their own track:

- Tap the Tracks button
- Tap the New Track button in bottom left

- Tap Audio Recorder
- Tap Voice
- Tap the Tracks button again
- Tap the track header and select 'Rename' to identify each track.

It may be helpful to turn off the sound of other tracks so they don't play during the new recording:

- Mute all other tracks, or
- Connect headphones to the iPad, or
- Turn off the iPad sound.

When recording:

- Select the appropriate track header for the next person
- Position the playhead AFTER the end of the last recorded clip
- Tap the Microphone button to return to the recording screen.

Muting tracks

When recording with a microphone into a **different track,** mute the existing tracks so they don't affect the next recording:

- Drag the handle in the middle of the left sidebar to the right to reveal the track volume controls, or tap the Track Controls button
- Tap the Speaker button (mute) to turn off the sound for that track – *it highlights blue when muted*

Editing the soundtrack

Now that you've recorded all the dialogue, it's time to select the best parts and edit them into a soundtrack.

Tap the Tracks button.

In this example, all the dialogue has been recorded in one track.

In this example, the dialogue for three characters has been recorded into three tracks.

To change the name of a track, tap twice on the track header and select Rename.

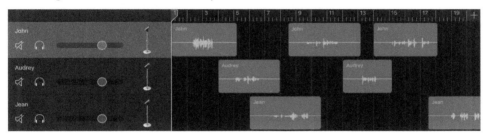

Use the pinch gesture as often as you need to zoom in or out to the level of magnification appropriate for each task.

Editing requires that the best clips are arranged to play in the right order and at the right time to create a seamless soundtrack. The basic editing tasks for dialogue are splitting, trimming and moving.

The first task is to remove unwanted recordings. If a number of takes are joined in the one clip **split** the clips, otherwise **trim** the clips to remove unwanted parts of recordings.

Splitting clips to keep the best parts

The first task is to remove any clips that you're not going to use. Listen to each sentence one at a time. If the clip has a mistake or was definitely not the best – delete it quick (double tap the clip and select 'Delete' from the list of editing options). **Don't move clips sideways to close up the gaps** just yet. If there is more than one good version, listen to them all and decide which is the best – often it will be the last one. If clips don't need splitting move on to the next task.

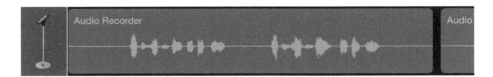

To split a clip:

- Tap the number scale above the middle of the gap between the versions ot "takes" (the middle of the recorded silence) to position the playhead – no need to drag it from its previous position

- Double tap the clip and select 'Split' from the list of editing options

- Drag the scissors – *they highlight yellow* – down to split the clip in two

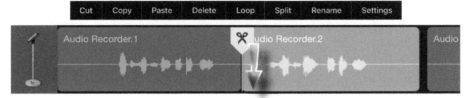

- Double tap on the unwanted part and select 'Delete' from the list of editing options.

Repeat splitting and discarding unwanted recording for every block of dialogue in every track.

Don't move clips sideways to close up gaps as that is an unnecessary step at the moment.

Trimming audio clips

An alternative editing method is to trim clips from each end.

- Use the pinch to zoom in for more accuracy

- Tap a clip – *it highlights yellow*

- Drag the solid bar at each end of the clip inwards to shorten it to the required length. Trim clips close to the start of the dialogue, but leave space at the end for natural falloff in sound, such as the last syllable or an echo.

Arranging clips in tracks and play order

If you recorded the dialogue in one track, this is a useful time to add another track which will allow better editing to create a continuous sound:

- Tap the New track button (+) in the bottom left
- Tap the Audio Recorder instrument
- Tap Voice
- Tap the Tracks button to return to the Tracks screen
- Use the pinch to zoom out if necessary
- Drag every second clip downwards into the new track.

To select several clips, tap and hold one clip then tap additional clips.

The first part of most movies is the title. (Adapt these instructions to suit if you want your title elsewhere, such as after the first line of dialogue):

- **Drag the first clip along its track so the dialogue starts after five seconds** to allow for the title – approximately 3 bars on the Timeline. This clip becomes the 'anchor' for the soundtracks – all other clips will flow from this

The numbers across the top of the tracks are musical bars which are different to seconds.

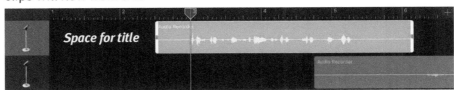

- Drag the other clips along the tracks so they play at the right time. Some dialogue should flow like a conversation. Some dialogue needs a gap to allow for actions or scene changes. Don't make gaps too long as **every extra second requires additional animation pictures.** A shorter soundtrack will often be better.

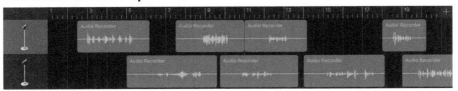

Trimming clips to remove noise

In general, trimming clips to leave just the dialogue will make the soundtrack cleaner.

Now that clips are in their final position check the trimming of each clip.

If the clips have noise in the background the ends of the clips will cut to silence and draw attention to themselves.

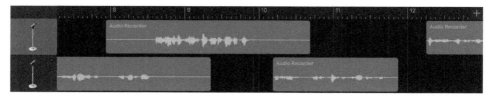

Disguise background noise by trimming clips (tap, then drag the solid bar at each end), where possible, to a point where there is sound in another track.

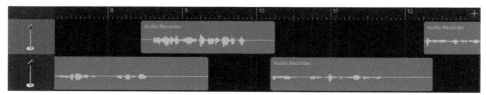

Adding effects

Effects can be applied to any Audio Recording track.

Effects apply to the entire track. If you need some clips with an effect and some clips without, spread the clips over several tracks and then apply the effect to the appropriate track.

To add an effect to an Audio Recording track:

- From the Tracks screen tap the track
- Tap the Microphone button at the top

- Swipe or tap the Narrator picture to use different types of microphones,
  or
  adjust the controls at the bottom to vary the effect,
  or
  tap the Fun button at the top
- Listen to the effect to make sure the sound is still clear.

Only one effect can be applied to a track at a time. However, when the track is merged the effect is locked in and another effect can be applied.

Swipe the Narrator picture to see different types of microphones. These settings do not change the recording itself, but apply an effect such as an echo. These settings can also be changed later.

Effects can also be applied to other types of instrument tracks if they are first merged, ie converted to an Audio Recorder track (see *Editing tracks* on page 94). Merging tracks means they can no longer be edited as instruments, so duplicate the original instrument track to keep a copy of it or apply the effect at the last stage.

Reverb

Reverb is an effect that overrides the starkness of the natural voice by smoothing it to produce a fuller sound. To add reverb to a track tap the Track Controls button.

A small amount of reverb is useful for most dialogue. Whereas a large amount of reverb for particular dialogue turns it into a booming stadium.

 To hear an example of dialogue, go to:
www.ipadanimation.net/epub_media2.html

Adding sound effects

Sound effects provide realism to the soundtrack to help convey that the story is really happening. A sound effect can be:

- A particular sound such as a knock at the door or a car crash
- A quiet underlying ambience of the sounds at the location such a park or cafe
- An actual audible event such as a phone ring or someone snoring
- To add emphasis such as a woosh of light or a bass stab of a heartbeat.

Most soundtracks will benefit from the addition of at least one sound effect. Adding a large number of appropriate sound effects can create a rich soundtrack as long as the story dialogue remains clear.

The quickest way to add a sound effect may be to record your own. So if you need a door slam, ticking clock, fingernail scraping across a board or someone snoring, use the same method for recording dialogue:

- Add a new Audio Recorder track – third track
- **Make sure the playhead is AFTER the end of the last recorded clip**
- Record the sound (see *Sound recording process* on page 46)
- In the Tracks screen, trim the clip then drag it along the track to the right place.

GarageBand has a selection of sound effects. Search *'FX'* in the Loop panel, or select the Genre 'Sound Effects'

Use iTunes playlists to make it easier to locate the sound effect you want:

- In the Tracks screen tap the Loop button

- Tap Music and locate the sound effect
- Drag the sound effect into an empty part of the track designated for sound effects (eg track 3) or into the space below the tracks to create a new track
- Drag the sound effect clip along the track to the right place.

You can add several sound effects into the same track.

Getting additional sound effects and music

Make sure you've downloaded all the available loops and sounds for GarageBand. Tap Loops, then tap Go to Sound Library.

To get the best sound effects and music for your stop motion search for *free* or *royalty-free* sound effects/ music.

For information on a wide range of sources for sound effects and music go to *www. stop-motion-handbook.com/ pages/audio_resources.html*

Creating sound effects

There are two ways to record sound effects with the microphone – Audio Recorder and Sampler:

The volume level of sound effects should not overpower the clarity of the dialogue. We'll adjust the volume at the end.

	Audio Recorder	Sampler
Add effects, eg distortion	•	
Add echo/reverb	•	•
Change pitch		•
Tune sound		•
Change volume shape		•
Play backwards		•
Save to GarageBand library		•
Transpose track		•

The soundtrack on the previous page used a sound effect for a sliding door on a spacecraft. This is how it was created with the Audio Recorder:

Space door open

- Place a piece of paper on the table next to the microphone
- Tap Record
- About 5cm from the microphone, heavily drop three fingers onto the paper and drag the paper towards you
- Tap the Stop button to end recording
- Tap the Track Controls button and add 30% reverb.

To hear hand-slide sound effects, go to:
www.ipadanimation.net/epub_media2.html

Sound effects reference

An excellent reference for recording sound effects is *'The Sound Effects Bible'* by Ric Viers. It is written for big screen movie makers, but it contains many useful ideas to create your own sounds effects with everyday items such as food.

55

Adding music

Music creates identity for your stop motion. **Right from the start of your movie it can set the tone of the story,** so take care to choose the right type of music.

These are some of the different types of music which are used for different purposes:

- **Theme tune** – a full length tune which adds a unique feel to the stop motion. It is important to choose an appropriate tune. In a short stop motion the title music needs to be up to ten seconds long before the first dialogue is spoken. The volume may need to be reduced when there is dialogue

- **Stinger** – a very short tune useful at the start of a scene, between scenes, or to draw attention

- **Underscore** – a quiet tune designed to play under dialogue

- **Loop** – a short tune designed to repeat without creating an obvious join

- **Atmosphere (ambience or soundscape)** – long recording of the sounds heard in a particular location such as at a park, cafe, train station or in space.

Quiet background music disguises ambient noise in the voice recording. It also helps to lift the 'apparent' quality of the voices.

Where to get music

- GarageBand installs a large selection of music loops and you can download more through the Loops button - tap Go to Sound Library

- Use instrumental music from your iTunes library. Create a playlist of useful music so it will be easier to locate the one you want

- Search for *free* or *royalty-free* music. For a list of excellent sites for sound effects we've used go to *Getting sound effects and music* on page 34, or go to *www.stop-motion-handbook.com/pages/audio_resources.html*

- Create your own music using the instruments in GarageBand (see *Recording Music* on page 73).

Don't use popular music from the radio or YouTube because the words make it hard to fit in with your dialogue. Also, it's illegal.

In this section we'll use existing music (loops and audio files) as background music.

Apple Loops

The obvious benefit of loops is they can be repeated (looped) without an audible join therefore creating a continuous sound of any length.

The pitch and tempo of loops automatically change according to the setting for the song. This is a big advantage over audio files and music which have fixed pitch and tempo.

To add loops:

- Tap the Loop button in the top right to see the available loops and music

- Tap Apple loops (Audio Files and Music panels only appear if the iPad has that type of content)

- Scroll through the list using the letter index on the right or narrow the selection by typing a keyword or specifying the Instrument, Genre or Descriptors

- Tap the name to listen to it

- Drag the loop into the space below the tracks – *a new Audio Recorder track is automatically added.*

Loops automatically repeat to fill the track to the end, but can be trimmed to make them shorter. Several different loops or files can be added to the same track.

Fill the entire length of the soundtrack with loops or music to suit the moods in different parts of the story (see tracks 4 and 5).

Use silence (no music) as an effect to add impact to part of the story.

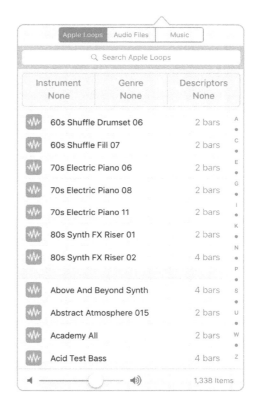

After the last dialogue, continue the music for at least five seconds to allow for the credits.

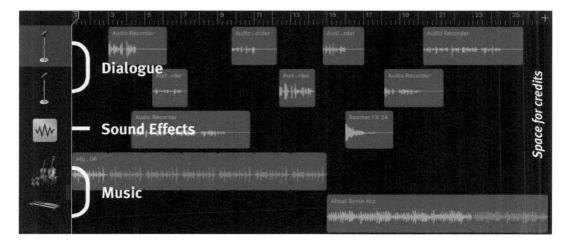

Audio Files

Audio Files (also called GarageBand documents) are music, soundtracks and sound effects available to GarageBand (see *Transferring a song via iTunes* on page 100).

Files can be in AIFF, WAV, CAF, Apple Loops, AAC, MP3 or M4A formats. GarageBand uses the M4A format when exporting songs in the iTunes format. This format lets you bring one GarageBand song into a different song.

Audio files are placed once in the track. Double tap the clip to loop it.

The files with the suffix 'band' have been saved in the GarageBand format. They can't be inserted into a GarageBand song, but can be opened in GarageBand on the iPad or Mac.

Music

Search for music from the iPad's music library by albums, artists, genres, playlists or song name. **Use iTunes playlists to make it easier to find the music you want to use.**

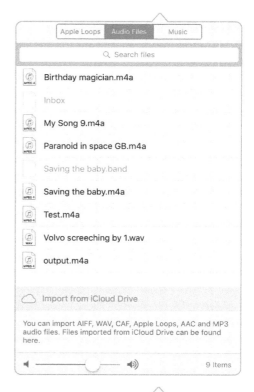

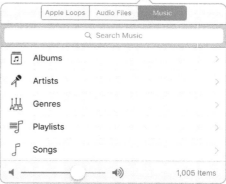

Adjusting the volume

In this chapter we have focussed on recording clean sound clips and arranging them to play at the right time. The final consideration to produce the best overall sound balance is adjusting the volume of each track.

There are two ways to adjust the volume: **track volume,** which adjusts the whole track, and **automation,** which changes the volume to different parts of a track.

Adjusting track volumes

Drag the handle in the middle of the track header (left side) towards the right to reveal the track volume controls.

Adjust the volume for each track as required. Make sure the dialogue can be heard clearly above the sound effects and music.

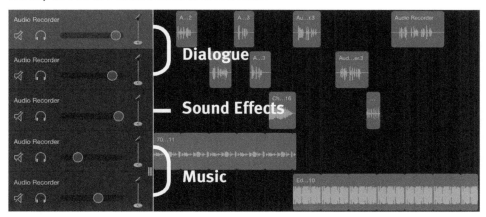

If some dialogue voices are too quiet or too loud create a new Audio Recorder track for the clip and give that track a different volume level.

Adjust volume with track automation

Sometimes you need to change the volume within a track, eg a siren starts loud but then needs to quieten off to allow dialogue to be heard:

Adjust volume last because the automation line does not move if you move the clip along the track.

• Tap a track header (left side) then tap it again to see the track editing options

- Select Automation

- Slide the pen button (top left) to unlock the tracks – *it highlights red*

- Tap on the volume line in the track where you want to change the volume – *it highlights yellow*

- Drag the edit point up or down to change the volume at that point

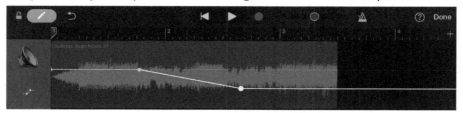

- To remove an edit point, tap again on the point and select Delete.

You can play the song at any time to listen to the effect of your changes.

When you are finished, tap Done in the top right.

Finishing the soundtrack

Listen to the complete soundtrack and think about what the animation should look like:

- Is there enough music at the start for the title? *If not, double tap on an empty part of the track and select 'Select all'. Touch and drag a clip along the track. Tap to deselect the clips. Extend the music at the start*

- Is there enough time for the actions between parts of dialogue? *If not, move the relevant clips along the track*

- Is the dialogue easy to hear above the sound effects and music? *If not, adjust the track volume*

- Is there enough music at the end for the credits? *If not, extend the music at the end.*

For more advanced editing, see *Editing tracks* on page 92.

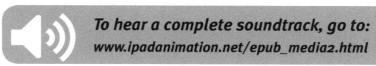

To hear a complete soundtrack, go to:
www.ipadanimation.net/epub_media2.html

Saving the soundtrack

Tap My Songs in the top left – this also saves the file.

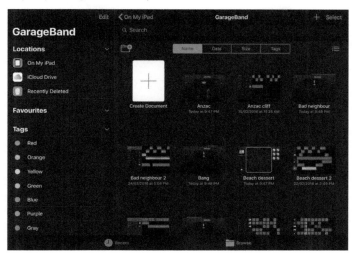

The completed soundtrack is useful in many situations requiring an audio file, such as on the radio, to accompany a play or performance or a Podcast.

However, our goal for this book is to create stop motion so we'll send the soundtrack to iStopMotion where we'll add the pictures:

- Each song (soundtrack) has a thumbnail picture with a name, designated *'My Movie X'* until you rename it. It is a good habit to rename songs to avoid confusion. Tap on the name and type a name to identify the soundtrack
- Tap the Select button in the top right
- Tap the soundtrack you've just made – *it highlights blue*
- Tap the Share button in the bottom left
- Tap 'Song' format

- Enter your name as the artist

61

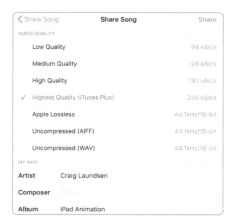

Choose the audio quality – in general choose one of the higher quality options

- Tap Share in the top right
- Scroll through the icons to tap Copy to iStopMotion, or tap Open In... and select Copy to iStopMotion – *iStopMotion automatically opens and the soundtrack is added.*

We will continue with iStopMotion after we've built the set.

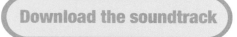

Find the original GarageBand file and the MP3 of this soundtrack in the download.

WELL DONE!

You've completed the soundtrack for a story-driven stop motion.
The next steps are: Build the set *(page 111)*, **then Record the pictures**
(page 147)

RECORDING SAMPLES

Making your own groove

Sampling is recording little clips of sound and using them in a completely different context to produce a new sound. Samples can create unique sound effects or new musical instruments.

 **Watch a stop motion with sampled sounds:**
www.ipadanimation.net/epub_media2.html

A number of attributes of sampled sounds can be changed such as pitch, volume and tuning. These can dramatically alter the dynamics of the sound so that it often becomes unrecognisable from the original recording.

- From the My Songs screen tap the New Song button (+) or the Create Document button
- Swipe left or right through the Instrument Browser until you see Keyboard

63

- Tap the Sampler button.

Recording a soundtrack with the Sampler is a two stage process:

- First – **record the samples**
- Second – **record the soundtrack** using the samples.

Recording samples

The Sampler will make a sound effect or instrument from almost anything, such as:

- A squeaking gate or door
- Shutting a car door
- Cracking an egg
- Turning a key in a door
- Clicking fingers
- Turning a pepper grinder
- Flipping through pages of a book
- Pouring dry cereal into a bowl
- Brushing teeth
- Crinkling an empty aluminium drink can
- Banging a saucepan lid with hand or hard object
- Cutting with scissors
- Pouring water from one glass to another

- Spoken words or sounds.

Before recording samples:

- Find the quietest space you can (see *Sound versus noise* on page 40)
- Make sure you know how to use a microphone (see *Using a microphone* on page 37)
- Place the iPad microphone about 30cm from the sound source
- Practise making the sound and watch the bars on the input level. The bars should rise to almost reach the top of the column. If they don't rise very high, make the sound louder or move the microphone closer. If they reach the top and stay there for a while the sound will be distorted so move the microphone away.

When you are ready to record the sample:

- Tap the Start button. If there is no discernible ambient noise the recording will only actually start when a distinct sound is heard. If there is noise (eg hum, wind, chatter) the recording may start immediately
- Make the sound. You only need the sound of one hit, shake or splash for each sample. Record several repetitions of the sound and choose the best one.

  Try recording a sample while holding the object and again with the object on a table. Some objects have a handle and can hang freely. You want the cleanest, purest sound including any ringing, resonance or echo, but not secondary noises such as the object scraping on the table

- Tap the Stop button

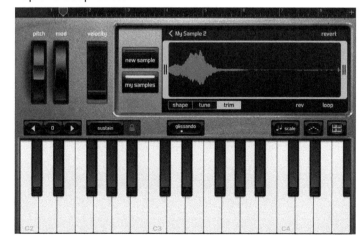

- Tap the Trim button under the picture of the sound shape

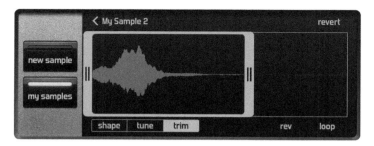

- Drag the bold bars at each end of the recording inwards to trim the recording so the sound starts immediately. Touch and hold the bars and the scale will increase so you can trim more accurately.

Using existing audio as a sample

If the sound you want to use as a sample is part of an existing audio file (Apple loop, audio file or music library):

- Tap the Import button in the top right
- Select the audio
- Tap the add button.

If the sound you want to use as a sample has been recorded in an Audio Recorder track or a Guitar Amp track, in the Tracks screen drag the clip into a Sampler track to use it as a sample.

Testing a sample

Short sounds are better for use as an instrument. If the sound is a longer recording such as slurping liquid, experiment with trimming the sound to the start or end.

Play note C3 and the sample will sound like the original. For each other note, the pitch will be adjusted to make the sound higher or lower. If the sound is to be played lower (deeper) make sure the sample is recorded with good volume to counter the natural volume decrease.

Use the Sustain slide switch to play the entire sound, or hold the note and wait until it has finished to achieve the same outcome.

Sampling a sound effect

We'll sample the sound of cutting a piece of paper to create a sound effect that could be used as a heavy door opening:

- Open the Sampler

- Place a piece of paper very close to the microphone (around 5cm)
- Tap the Start button and record a sample of a single cut with scissors. Take care to ensure silence before and after the sound and to avoid secondary noises such as the scissors making contact with the table
- Tap the Record button and play note C1 (two octaves lower pitch)
- In Tracks screen, tap the track header twice
- Select 'merge' convert the track into an Audio Recorder track
- Tap the microphone icon to apply the Bullhorn effect with a little distortion.

Here are some other examples of sound effects created from samples (the original sound plays first):

- **Ominous** – a recording of happy kids cheering (note C3) turns into a haunted scene at a much lower pitch (note C0)
- **Thunder** – vinegar shaken in a bottle turns into thunder and stormy weather at a lower pitch (note C0)
- **Monster** – the word spoken is "I'm". Choose words without hard consonants such as "T, C, K", or thin hissy sounds such as "S". Human speech samples sound normal around the note C3. At a much lower pitch (note C0) will sound like a deep rumbling monster
- **Alien speech** – record a full sentence and play it back at the same pitch (note C3). The 'Rev' option plays the sound backwards. This could be a way to create your own alien speech or a foreign language. Play the sample back one or two notes higher or lower for a variation.

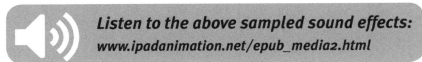

Listen to the above sampled sound effects:
www.ipadanimation.net/epub_media2.html

Sound shape and tune

Tap the Shape button to see the sound curve. This determines how quickly the sound reaches full volume and quietens down.

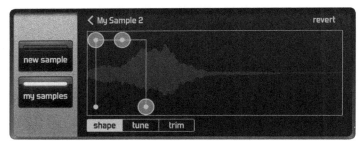

The sound in the above shape is at full volume at the start. This is called the 'attack'. The sound then quietens off very quickly. This is called the 'decay'. This produces a very quick, sharp sound.

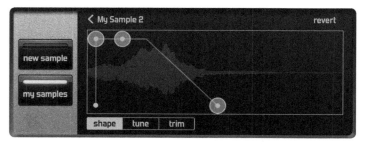

The sound in the above shape has a quick start and then tails off slowly. This is a more normal sound shape.

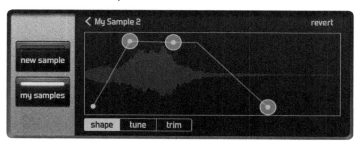

The sound in the above shape gradually gets louder, like an approaching train, and gradually quietens off.

Melodic sounds can be tuned so the sample matches the pitch of a note played on an actual musical instrument. This could turn a series of clangs into an instrument. To tune a sample tap 'tune', and while playing the same note on the iPad and the real instrument, slide the course tune slider, and then the fine tune slider, until the notes sound the same.

When you have finished adjusting your sample, tap the 'My Sample X' button:

- If you only want to use the sample with this song, tap the Rename button and type a name for the sample, or

- If you want to use the sample in other songs, tap 'add to library', and type a name for the sample.

Sampling a song

In the rest of this chapter we are going to record an entire song using just samples. The goal for this soundtrack is to record samples from sounds found in one place – *we used sounds from the kitchen.*

Bass sounds

Find a large solid object to produce deep sounds. If the sound is low and quiet move the microphone closer to record a good loud sample, such as:

- Tapping the skin of a whole watermelon.

Rhythm (percussion type) sounds

Almost anything can be played like a drum. We are looking for a range of interesting and different sounds:

- Shaking olive oil in bottle
- Sliding a wooden spoon over metal cheese grater
- Shaking a salt shaker
- Hitting a metal cheese grater with a wooden spoon.

Melody sounds

Look for objects which have a hollow shape, such as a bowl or dish. Round shapes have a deeper sound. Glass, ceramic and plastic bowls will produce different sounds. Tap the bowl using a range of methods: finger tap, finger flick, wooden stick and metal utensil. Try an empty bowl and also partly filled with liquid. Sounds with a pure ring will have good musical properties when played back at a different pitch:

- Tapping a salad bowl.

Human sounds

As this is a happy song, we recorded a person making party mood sounds:

- *"Woo"* (recorded as one word, but will be played as two notes one after the other)
- *"Doot"* (recorded as one word, but will be played as a run of three different notes).

Go to the link below to hear the samples we recorded (playing in this order – tap watermelon, shake olive oil bottle, slide wooden spoon on cheese grater, salt shaker, hit salad bowl, say "woo", say "doot", hit cheese grater).

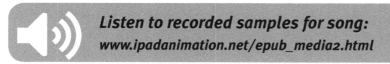

Listen to recorded samples for song:
www.ipadanimation.net/epub_media2.html

Using samples

When you have recorded the samples and are ready to create a 'song':

- Tap My Samples
- Tap the name of the sample you want to use

- Play notes on the keyboard to hear the sampled sound in different pitches
- The three buttons on the left change the notes to a higher or lower octave

- The Sustain slide button determines how quickly the sound fades away

- The Arpeggiator button gives a fuller melody by playing a sequence of the sample at a higher and lower pitch.

We created several tracks for a rhythm, starting with a repeating 'tap tap' on a watermelon.

Sampler instruments are electronic are don't use the microphone, so use the metronome when creating a song – *it should be blue*. This will help each new sample play in time as you build up the complete sound.

When you are ready to record:

- Set Sections to Automatic
- Make sure the playhead is at the start
- Tap the Record button (red dot)

- Wait for the four beat count-in
- Play the notes to produce the sounds, tune or rhythm
- Tap the Stop button to end recording.

Each track can only use one sample. To record another sample:

- Tap the Tracks button

- Tap the New Track button (plus sign in bottom left)

+

- Tap the Sampler in the Instrument Browser
- Record the sample.

To hear an individual track:

- Drag the handle in the middle of the left side bar to the right to reveal the track volume controls
- Tap the headphone button on that track.

If you need to edit the tracks, see *Editing songs* on page 91.

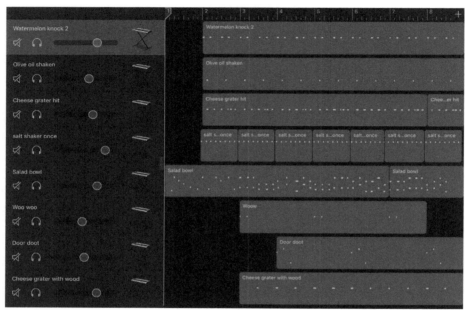

When you have finished your song:

- Tap the My Songs button to save your song
- Tap on the name *'My Song X'* and type your name to identify it.

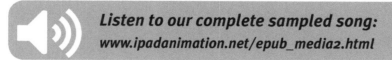

Listen to our complete sampled song:
www.ipadanimation.net/epub_media2.html

Download the soundtrack

Find the original GarageBand file and the MP3 of this soundtrack in the download.

Recording music

GarageBand is packed full of musical possibilities. It is useful for creating background music or theme tunes, whether you are making a soundtrack for a movie or an actual song.

GarageBand music is for the musician, and with assistance of this chapter, the non-musician. It has many smart and automatic features to assist everyone to produce a tune.

All Garageband instruments, have smart and automatic features to help you create a unique song, regardless of your musical ability. Take the time to experiment and have fun with the wide range of sounds. When you are ready to record, follow the steps in this section to construct a song.

GarageBand displays controls for each instrument, or you can connect a MIDI keyboard or guitar to the iPad and use a musical instrument.

A musical soundtrack has one instrument per track. We'll use four tracks.

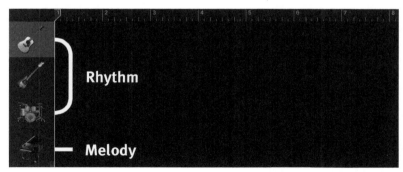

Remember, there are many ways to put a 'song' together – the example in this chapter is just one of them. In general, you need to create a rhythm and a melody:

- **Rhythm** – an underlying texture – a base layer – an accompaniment. GarageBand's smart instruments and automatic features allow you to quickly put together quite sophisticated sounds. A rhythm might include several tracks with different instruments, such as drums and bass. You can have more than one track for the same instrument to achieve different effects

73

- **Melody** to personalise the song. This can be as simple as a one finger tune using automatic features such as chords and the Arpeggiator to add extra notes for you. If you are a musician you may want to turn off the automatic features and compose something original.

It is a matter of choice and experimentation whether you record the rhythm first (to help keep all the parts of the music in time), and then add a melody, or if you have a tune in mind record the melody first, then create a rhythm to go with it.

The tuning and range of notes offered by GarageBand instruments is called the 'key'. GarageBand starts in the key of C. This can be changed in Song Settings.

Create a four-track music tune

Follow the steps in this chapter to create a musical tune.

- From the My Songs screen tap the New Song button

The first instrument (guitar)

We will create the rhythm first, starting with the guitar as it is tuneful and might lead to a melody. For a different song we might start with drums to establish a good beat.

- Swipe left or right to until you see Guitar

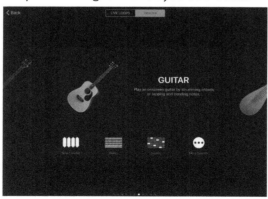

- Tap Smart Guitar button

- Tap the picture of a guitar to choose the type of sound. We'll use the *Acoustic*.

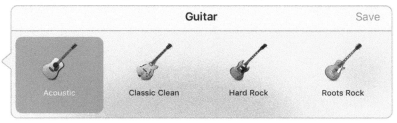

To play the guitar tap the chord strips. Tap with two or three fingers for variations.

Autoplay

Each smart instrument has Autoplay options which help to create musical sounds. With Autoplay, you won't need to tap many notes because automatic rhythms have patterns or cycles which carry the rhythm texture. We'll use *Autoplay setting 4*.

The Chords/Notes switch changes the instrument between a simple chord base or actual strings to play like a real guitar including tap to pluck a note, and drag to bend a note. We'll use *chords*.

GarageBand instruments are electronic and don't use the microphone, so use the metronome when creating a rhythm:

- Tap the Metronome button to turn it ON – *it should be blue*

- Next, tap the Song Settings button in the top right

- The 4 beat count-in is generally useful for music, so turn this on

- Lastly, tap the Sections button (plus sign) in the top right

- Tap on the number next to Section A and turn ON Automatic section length.

When you are ready to record:

- Make sure the playhead is at the start
- Tap the Record button (red dot)

- Wait for the four beat count-in
- Tap the screen to 'play' the guitar. To follow our example, tap these notes just **before** each bar number:

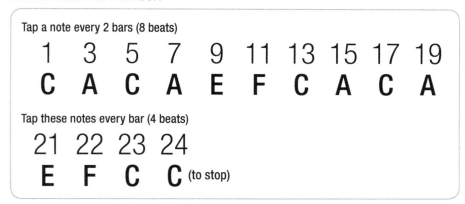

Tap a note every 2 bars (8 beats)

1	3	5	7	9	11	13	15	17	19
C	A	C	A	E	F	C	A	C	A

Tap these notes every bar (4 beats)

21	22	23	24
E	F	C	C (to stop)

- Tap the Stop button to end recording.

If you make a mistake, make sure the playhead is at the start and record again. This will erase the first one and record a replacement.

Auto correction

GarageBand has an option to automatically correct notes to the timing of the song:

- Tap the Track Controls button

- Tap Track Settings
- Tap Quantisation
- Tap Straight and 1/16 Note. This is the best option for this track because the Autoplay option we used has lots of very short notes in every beat.

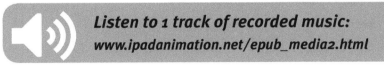

Listen to 1 track of recorded music:
www.ipadanimation.net/epub_media2.html

See also *Advanced guitar for musicians* on page 88.

Add another instrument (bass)

Tap the Instrument Browser button to choose the next instrument:

- Swipe left or right until you see Bass. This instrument will add some deeper tones to the rhythm of the guitar

- Tap Smart Bass

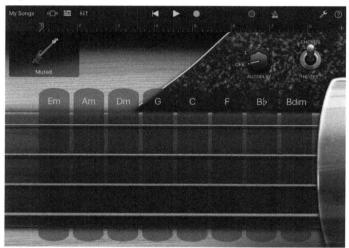

- Tap the picture of a bass to choose the type of sound. We'll use *Muted*

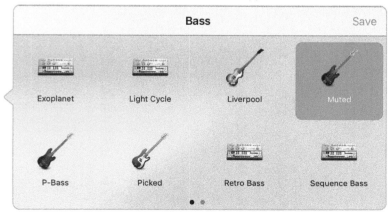

78

- Tap the Chord strips to play the bass. Tap with two or three fingers for variations to the rhythm.

The Chords/Notes switch changes the instrument between a simple chord base or actual strings to play like a bass guitar including tap to pluck a note, and drag to bend a note. We'll use *chords* and *Autoplay setting 1*.

The bass will be recorded in a second track, separate to the guitar. As you record the bass, you will hear the guitar in the first track to help keep the music in time as it starts to build up to a complete song.

When you are ready to record:

- Make sure the playhead is at the start
- Tap the red Record button and wait for the count-in
- Tap the screen to 'play' the bass. To follow our example:

Tap a note every 2 bars (8 beats)

1	3	5	7	9	11	13	15	17	19
C	A	C	A	E	F	C	A	C	A

Tap these notes every bar (4 beats)

21	22	23	24
E	F	C	C (to stop)

You may notice this is the same sequence used for the first track. A simple strategy for creating music is to use the same note sequence on different rhythm instruments

- Tap the Stop button to end recording.

Tap the Tracks button for an overall view of the recording and to see how each instrument fits with the others.

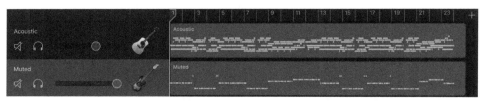

Tap the Track Controls button and turn on Quantisation to 1/8 Note as the bass has less fill-in notes.

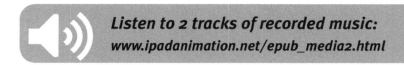

Listen to 2 tracks of recorded music:
www.ipadanimation.net/epub_media2.html

Listen for the bass. It will be quiet, but it adds a layer of deeper notes for a richer sound. **The deeper sound will be more obvious through headphones or connect the iPad to bigger speakers which produce better bass sounds.**

To hear an individual track:

- Drag the handle in the middle of the left side bar to the right to reveal the track volume controls

- Tap the headphone button on that track.

See also *Advanced guitar for musicians* on page 88.

Add another instrument (drums)

Tap the Instrument Browser to choose the next instrument:

- Swipe left or right to until you see Drums.

As the drums are being added third, it will be easier to find a beat which fits with the instruments already recorded. For other soundtracks, the drums might be recorded first but an ambitious beat might make it harder to add other instruments

- Tap Smart Drums

- Tap the picture of a drum kit (upper left) to choose the type of sound. We'll use *Live Rock Kit.*

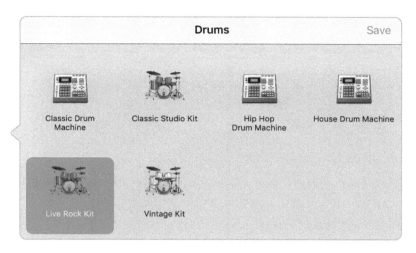

Smart Drums use a priority grid to automatically create rhythms. And because they are a smart instrument they automatically fit with the other instruments.

Drums placed near the TOP of the grid play louder and those near the BOTTOM play quieter.

Drums placed near the LEFT of the grid have simple beats and those near the RIGHT have more complex beats.

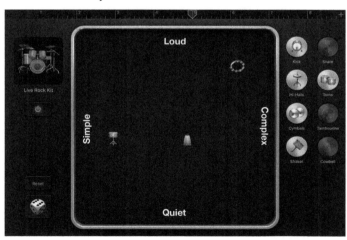

The various components from the selected drum kit are either placed on the grid or waiting on the side.

To vary the rhythm, drag drum pieces on or off the grid and around the grid, or tap the dice to randomise the drum arrangement. This allows you to customise the rhythm for different parts of the song, but the 'smart' part of the drums automatically keeps it all in time and sounding good. Tap the dice as often as you want (even every bar) to create an original drum track.

Tap the on button – *it highlights blue* – to hear the drums as you arrange the rhythm.

Copy the above smart drum set up to follow our example.

When you are ready to record:

- Make sure the playhead is at bar 5. We are going to start the drums after the guitar has complete one full cycle of its rhythm
- Tap the red Record button. The drums will automatically play the sound and rhythm you've chosen
- Tap the Stop button to end recording.

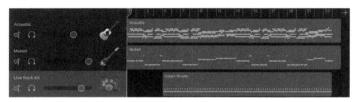

Adjust the volume for each track to produce a balanced overall sound.

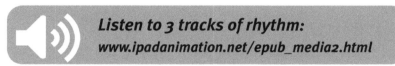

Listen to 3 tracks of rhythm:
www.ipadanimation.net/epub_media2.html

For an alternative drum track you could use the Drummer instrument. It uses the same type of grid method, but has more options to create a customised beat.

See also *Advanced drums for musicians* on page 90.

Add the melody (piano)

The rhythm is now complete, so to finish off the song we need to personalise it with a melody. We'll use a keyboard. If you want to listen to the melody before playing it yourself, follow the link at the end of this section:

- Tap the Instrument Browser.

  Because the melody needs to be a distinct tune, we are going to use a real keyboard. If you are not a musician, you may want to get someone to help you with this part. The simpler version of the music is very easy, so listen to the finished song and you may be able to play the tune yourself. We'll cover the Smart keyboard at the end of this section

- Swipe left or right until you see Keyboard

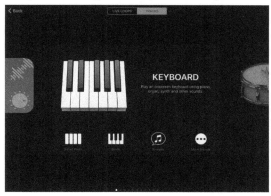

- Tap Synth
- Tap the small picture of the type of keyboard
- Tap Keyboards and select Grand Piano
- Tap Done.

The Keyboard has many more sounds than the Smart Keyboard. We'll use the *Grand Piano*. If you are using the keyboard on the screen, set the *octave range to +1*.

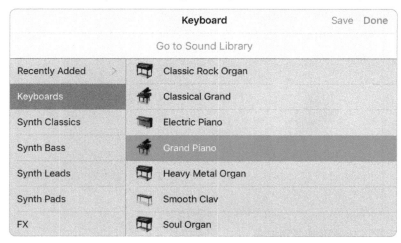

The keyboard is one instrument where it may be easier to use a real instrument. Connect a real keyboard to the iPad with the USB Camera Adapter.

The keyboard starts in the 5th bar at the same time as the drums.

- Tap the red Record button. Listen to the first four bars and be ready to start playing in bar 5

- 'Play' the melody. Our song only needs a simple melody that can be played with one finger – on the opposite page are two versions of the music to suit different musical abilities. To follow our example the starting note is C3

Simpler

Better

- Tap the Stop button to end recording.

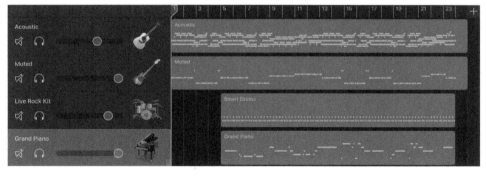

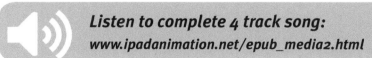

Listen to complete 4 track song:
www.ipadanimation.net/epub_media2.html

Download the soundtrack

Find the original GarageBand file and the MP3 of this soundtrack in the download.

85

Alternative melody

When you change the instrument for the melody from the keyboard to Smart Guitar it produces a different type of sound. Mute the piano (track 4) and record the alternative melody in track 5.

Track 5: Smart Guitar using *Classic Clean* sound with *Heavenly Chorus* and *Blue Echo* effects. This is played as notes using taps and the occasional drag effect to bend a note.

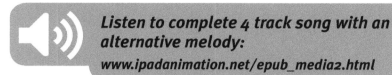

Listen to complete 4 track song with an alternative melody:

www.ipadanimation.net/epub_media2.html

Finishing off

If your song requires vocals for singing or talking, select an Audio Recorder track or add a new Audio Recorder track (tap Voice) and follow the steps from the earlier example. When recording with the microphone, use headphones so you can hear the music to help you to stay in time but it is not audible in the room where it would be re-recorded by the microphone.

If your song requires pre-recorded music or loops, see *Adding music* on page 56.

Edit the tracks in your song if necessary (see *Editing tracks* on page 92).

When you have finished your song:

- Tap the My Songs button to save your song
- Tap on the name *'My Song X'* and type your name to identify it.

Exploring other instruments

Smart piano

The smart piano offers intelligent and automated ways to help musicians and non-musicians create keyboard sounds very quickly. The smart piano is not suitable for the melody for this example, but is a great instrument as part of a rhythm or for another song.

In the Instrument Browser:

- Swipe left or right to until you see the Keyboard

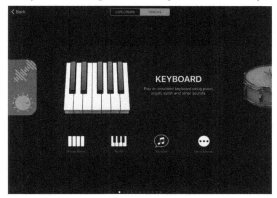

- Tap the Smart Piano.

When Autoplay is off, the keyboard is displayed as shown as below:

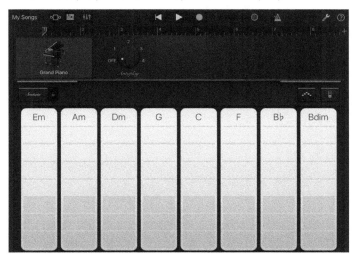

Tap on the five white spaces at the top of each note to play a **chord** in a different octave. The three shaded spaces at the bottom play a **note** in a different octave.

The Sustain switch holds the sound longer and smoothens the sound between notes.

The Arpeggiator adds a run of fill-in notes when you hold a note.

The other Autoplay settings simplify the keyboard further.

87

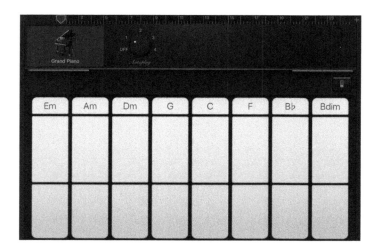

Advanced guitar for musicians

People who play guitar can connect a real guitar to the iPad using a connector such as Apogee Jam (pictured) or iRig:

- In the Instrument Browser, swipe left or right until you see Amp

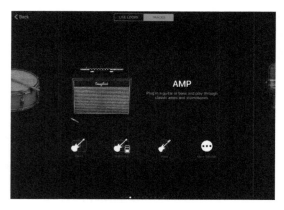

- Tap one of the buttons for a Clear, Distorted or Bass sound
- Tap the name at the top to choose the type of amplifier sound

- Adjust the sound using the controls on the amplifier
- Tap the Effects button to add stompbox effect modules.

Up to four large stompboxes are used as part of the current sound. The small pictures of stompboxes along the bottom are also available

- Tap in the large space to add a new stompbox, or tap on the large picture of the stompbox you want to replace or delete
- Tap the stompbox in the bottom row to add it to the current sound
- Adjust the stompbox controls to produce the desired sound
- Tap the Amplifier button to close the stompbox selection.

Advanced drums for musicians

If you are confident playing the drums, use the Drums.

- Tap Acoustic Drums
- Tap the drum kit name to select the drum sound.

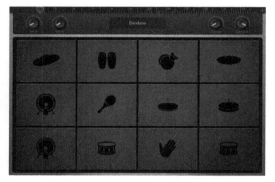

Playing the GarageBand drums is a matter of tapping the pictures of various drums and cymbals to create the sound. Tap the name of the drum kit to change the type of drums. Different parts of some drums make different sounds, eg tap on the rim of the snare drum for a rim shot.

If you want the benefits of the automated smart drums, but want to add an individual touch, create one track of Smart Drums, and a second track for the Acoustic Drums. As you play the drums you'll hear the sound of the smart drums to help keep it all in time.

90

EDITING SONGS

Once a track has been recorded, there are a number of ways the sound can be enhanced. These editing tasks range from a simple clean up of the recorded sounds to more comprehensive musical editing.

Track colours

The colour of a GarageBand track indicates how it was recorded, which determines how it can be edited:

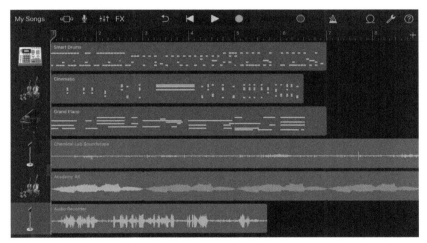

- **Green clips** – recorded musically from a built-in instrument or an instrument connected via USB. The notes are stored as MIDI (except for Smart Drums) and can be edited (see *MIDI editor* on page 94). Even though the original Sampler sounds are recorded with the microphone, the use and editing of these sounds is as a MIDI instrument.

  Track Controls includes two additional editing tools for MIDI tracks:

  – Quantisation (auto corrects notes to the timing of the song) and

  – Transposition (changes the entire track up or down to a different pitch)

- **Blue clips** – loops and audio files or recorded with the microphone. Tap on the current Instrument button to add a sound effect to change the characteristics of the sound.

Editing tracks

Tap an instrument picture to highlight the track. Tap again to see track editing options:

- **Delete** – delete the track
- **Duplicate** – create another track with the same instrument settings. If you want to duplicate the audio clips, see next page for 'copy' and 'paste' editing
- **Rename** – customise the name of the track to help with organising the tracks. If your soundtrack has a number of Audio Recorder tracks, it may be helpful to name the track with the name of the character

- **Merge** – combine several tracks into one. Tap on the circles next to the tracks you want to merge. Tap the Merge button at top right.

  Merging may be useful to combine tracks recorded with the microphone, such as lines of dialogue, but only after they have been finalised. Merging may also be a practical way to achieve more tracks in the song.

  Merged instrument tracks are converted to Audio Recorder tracks and are no longer editable as instruments

- **Automation** – change the volume within the track. This allows more flexibility than the track volume control (see *Adjust volume with track automation* on page 59).

If you need to change the order of the tracks, drag a track header up or down to a different position. This won't alter the sound, but reordering tracks can make it easier to understand the arrangement of your song.

The Undo button in the control bar will undo these actions.

Editing audio clips

Use the pinch to zoom in or out as often as you need to help you edit accurately.

- **Move** – drag the centre of an audio clip to a new position on that track. You can move clips into a different track that is the same instrument type

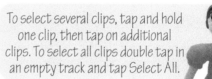

To select several clips, tap and hold one clip, then tap on additional clips. To select all clips double tap in an empty track and tap Select All.

- **Trim** – tap the audio clip, then drag the handles, at either end of the clip, to shorten it. Trimmed portions can be untrimmed later as they are just hidden, not deleted.

Double tap an audio clip to see the editing options:

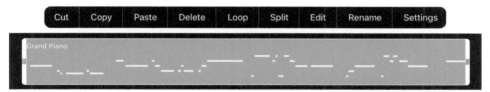

- **Cut** – remove the clip from the track but keep a copy in memory. Single tap an empty part of a track to access the option to paste it back

- **Copy** – copy the clip into memory so it can be pasted elsewhere. Tap on an empty part of any track of the same kind of instrument to access the option to paste it back

- **Paste** – if a clip from the same instrument as the current track has been copied, it will be pasted at the playhead. Copy and Paste can also be used to transfer clips between Garageband songs

- **Delete** – remove the clip

- **Trim** – when the clip is a loop, shorten either end of the first loop so it repeats more quickly

- **Loop** – fill the rest of the track by looping the clip

- **Split** – drag the scissors to the place you want to cut the track. Slide the scissors downward to split the clip into two pieces

- **Edit** – GarageBand records most of its instruments in a format called MIDI. This feature may be of more interest to people with some musical knowledge. MIDI means the notes are recorded in such a way that they can be changed afterwards. So if you've played a melody but made a small mistake, rather than replaying the entire piece again change individual notes, one at a time

- **Rename** – change the name of the clip to help with organising the song. You can change the clip name, but it is more useful to add extra information such as the actual words spoken

- **Settings** – depending on the type of instrument you can make adjustments such as transpose to a different key, change the speed, turn clips into loops and play the clip in reverse.

MIDI editor

Change or enhance individual notes in an instrument track. If the music note is wrong or was missed you can fix it without needing to replay the entire piece.

Even if you played 'note perfect', the sound can often be improved by adjusting the volume of some notes. For example, if the first note in a run is a bit quiet, make it louder so the melody starts confidently.

Don't try to make every aspect (timing, duration, volume) of every note perfect, as the overall sound may become clinically clean and lose its character.

- Double tap an audio clip to see if the Edit option is available for the instrument
- Tap Edit.

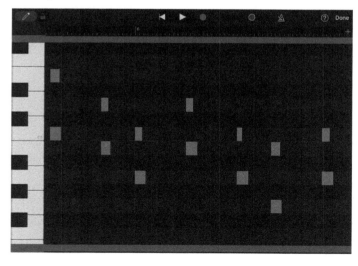

Use the pinch gesture to increase the scale horizontally and vertically so it is easier to make accurate editing adjustments.

- To **change the actual note,** drag the note vertically (this will fix that wrong note)
- To **change the timing,** drag the note horizontally
- To **change the duration,** drag the right end of the note
- To **change the volume,** tap the note to display the velocity option.

Tap Velocity and move the slider to the desired volume

- To **add a note,** slide the pen button (top left) to unlock the track – *it highlights red.*

Tap the screen to add the new note. Adjust the timing, duration and volume of the new note. When the pen button is active, tap a note to delete it.

At any stage, tap a note and it will play. Use the Play button in the control bar to play the track.

Use the Undo button at the top left if you make a mistake.

Drag the screen to move to a different part of the track.

Tap Done when you have finished editing.

Track Controls

Tap the Track Controls button to change the track volume and add effects such as echo and reverb.

The displayed controls are common to all tracks. Tap on the headings Track Settings, Plug-Ins and EQ and Master Effects for options specific to different instruments. For example tracks with green clips are MIDI notes, and have additional musical options.

Master Effects, at the bottom of the list, apply echo and reverb to the entire song.

Saving your song

- Tap the My Song button in the top left to save the song and close the screen
- Tap on the name *'My Song X'* and type your name to identify it.

Editing songs

The My Songs screen has several editing options:

- Tap the Select button in the top right
- Tap a song – *it highlights blue*
- Tap the appropriate editing button across the bottom.

Share – options for exporting the song (including exporting to YouTube, iMovie if installed on that iPad and iTunes). Until you share a song, it can only be played in GarageBand (see *Saving the soundtrack* on page 61). Even if the song has been shared, the original remains in GarageBand until it is deleted.

Duplicate – creates an exact copy of a song. This is useful if you want to make a different version of a song and keep the original version.

Move – Allows you to change the location for the song, such as to iCloud.

Delete – from time to time you will need to delete a song from GarageBand to free up space on your iPad. Make sure you have saved a copy to iTunes or another device before deleting it.

Transferring a GarageBand song to iStopMotion

One of the requirements of stop motion is to bring sound and pictures together. There are several ways to transfer a GarageBand song to another app such as iStopMotion or iMovie:

- **Open in...** [another app] is a direct method that is quick and easy
- **Airdrop** to share the files to another device
- via **iTunes** has more steps but allows more flexibility such as transferring songs to other devices which don't have Airdrop.

Open in...

If you have iStopMotion on your iPad, you can save a GarageBand song directly into the audio library in iStopMotion, from where it can be applied to a project.

If you have iMovie on your iPad, you can save a GarageBand song directly into an iMovie project.

Before transferring the song, make sure you have named it so it is easier to locate in future.

- Open iPad GarageBand's 'My Songs'
- Tap the Select button in the top right
- Tap the song you want to share – *it highlights blue*
- Tap the Share button in the bottom left
- Tap 'Song' format

- Select the quality for the audio - *at least high quality.*
  Enter your name as the artist

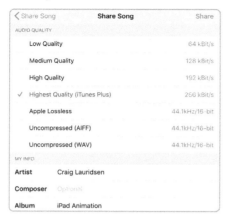

- Tap Share in the top right

Copy to iStopMotion

- Scroll through the icons to tap 'Copy to iStopMotion' or tap Open In... and select Copy to iStopMotion. The soundtrack is saved into the iStopMotion audio library

- In iStopMotion, open the stop motion project, tap the Audio button, and select the soundtrack (see *Adding a soundtrack* on page 157).

Copy to iMovie

This is particularly useful for larger stop motion projects that are to be assembled in iMovie. The process may easier if the iMovie project has already been created and given a unique name.

- Scroll through the icons to tap 'Copy to iMovie'

- Choose the iMovie project – a new iMovie project, the iMovie project that was last edited, or another existing iMovie project

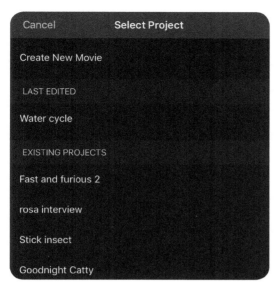

- If you select 'Create New Movie', a new iMovie project will open and the song will be added as background music in a green bar, ready to have the picture clips added

- If you select an iMovie project, it is opened:
  - Song more than 60 seconds long are added as background music (green bar)
  - Songs less than 60 seconds long are added at the playhead (blue bar). See *Adding sound* (iMovie Chapter) on page 192.

AirDrop

AirDrop shares files between devices with the Lightning charging connector. The devices do not need to share a WiFi connection. The receiving iPad will need the same version of Garageband, or later.

On the receiving iPad, flick up from the bottom of the screen and temporarily set AirDrop to 'Everyone'.

On the sending iPad:

- Open GarageBand's 'My Songs'
- **Name the song so it is easier to locate in future**
- Tap the Select button in the top right

- Tap the song you want to share – *it highlights blue*
- Tap the Share button in the bottom left
- If you want to allow editing on the other device tap 'Project'* otherwise tap 'Song' format

AirDrop

- Wait a few seconds until the AirDrop icon is replaced with a list of nearby devices
- Tap the name of the iPad you want to send the song to
- On the receiving iPad tap 'Accept' to receive the song.

*The fully editable GarageBand file is added to the My Songs screen in GarageBand. To add the GarageBand song to iStopMotion on the receiving iPad refer to earlier instructions for 'Open in...'.

Transferring a GarageBand song via iTunes on a computer

A third method for transferring a GarageBand file uses a computer. This may be a helpful method when you need to transfer to:

- an older iPad without a Lightning connector
- a Mac.

First we'll transfer the song from the iPad to the computer.

1) In iPad GarageBand, share the song via iTunes

- Open 'My Songs'
- **Name the song so it is easier to locate in future**
- Tap the Select button in the top right
- Tap the song you want to share – *it highlights blue*
- Tap the Share button in the bottom left
- Tap 'Song' format if you don't want to be able to further edit the song.

  Enter the artist information about the song if you wish. This information will make it easier to locate the song in future.

  Choose the audio quality – in general choose one of the higher quality options.

  Tap Share
- Alternatively, tap 'Project' format to save the song as fully editable GarageBand file.
- Tap Save to Files

via iTunes

Save to Files   Open in...   More

- Select the location to save the file such as 'On My iPad', then GarageBand, then, GarageBand File Transfer.
- Tap Add.

2) *Connect the iPad to the computer (it does not need to be the computer the iPad syncs to)*

- Open iTunes on the computer
- Select the iPad device
- Select the Apps tab
- Scroll to the File Sharing section at the bottom of the Apps window and select GarageBand in the list of Apps.

The GarageBand Documents panel includes songs that have been exported in iTunes format (shown as M4A or AIFF) or GarageBand format (.band).

3) *Save the GarageBand Document to the computer desktop*

- Select the song you want to transfer

- At the bottom of the window, click 'Save to...' and follow the prompts to save the music to the computer desktop. On a Mac, you can also drag the GarageBand song to the computer to achieve the same outcome

- Close the iPad window by selecting the Music window.

Transferring music from a computer to the iPad

If the soundtrack, such as GarageBand song, for your stop motion is on a computer, there are two ways to transfer it to the iPad:

Using the computer the iPad syncs to

- Select File⋯➔Add to Library and follow the prompts to add the audio files (AIFF, WAV, CAF, Apple Loops, AAC, MP3, or M4A format) into iTunes on your computer. On a Mac, you can also drag the song from the Finder back into iTunes to achieve the same outcome

- Create a playlist and add the song. **Creating a playlist will make it easier to locate your song.** Playlists are a good way to group all the songs, music and sounds you want to use when making soundtracks.

- Select the iPad device in iTunes

- Click on the Music tab, then click on the playlist containing the song you want to transfer

- Click Sync and eject the iPad.

The music is stored in the iPad's music library.

Using another computer

Add the music, soundtrack or sound effect as a GarageBand Document:

- Open iTunes on the computer
- **PC only** – select Edit┈▶Preferences and on the Devices tab deselect 'Prevent iPods, iPhones and iPads from syncing automatically'
- Connect the iPad to a computer
- Select the iPad device in iTunes
- Select the Apps tab
- Scroll to the File Sharing section at the bottom of the Apps window and select GarageBand in the list of Apps
- At the bottom of the GarageBand Documents window click 'Add...' and follow the prompts to add the audio file (AIFF, WAV, CAF, Apple Loops, AAC, MP3, M4A or band format). On a Mac, drag the audio file from the computer into the GarageBand Documents window. The file is immediately transferred to the iPad

- Click Done. **DO NOT CLICK SYNC**. Eject the iPad and disconnect.

Accessing GarageBand files on the iPad

- From the My Songs screen in GarageBand, select the Location 'On My iPad'

- Swipe one finger left or right, and up or down, to locate the song

- Tap on the song to open it.

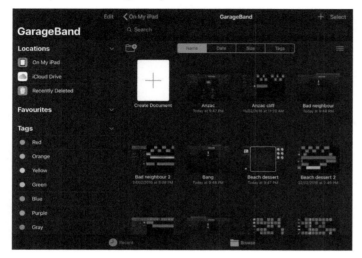

MIXING A SOUNDTRACK IN DJAY

Algoriddim's **djay** (App Store) **turns the iPad into a DJ system**.

Its particular relevance to stop motion is that it can save the recorded soundtrack directly into iStopMotion (or iMovie).

Whether you want a full DJ mix or have more modest audio requirements, djay might be all you need to make the soundtrack for your stop motion.

Record the soundtrack 'live' as you select the different audio files and adjust the settings.

Here are three scenarios for using djay to create a soundtrack:

Audio enhancement

In its simplest form, use djay to enhance an existing audio file. As it plays, make changes to volume or equaliser (EQ) effects to suit your requirements as you record a modified version.

You could also use djay to change the length and/or pitch of the audio file by adjusting the speed (beats per minute or BPM) (see *Tempo and pitch* on page 108).

Combining audio files

iStopMotion soundtracks need to be a single audio file. So if you have several audio files, eg one for the title, a background tune and a sound effect to use at the climax, use djay to combine these into one audio file. Blend the different files together and adjust the volume or EQ effects to suit your requirements.

Full DJ mix

Go to *www.algoriddim.com* for tutorials on making the most of the features of djay.

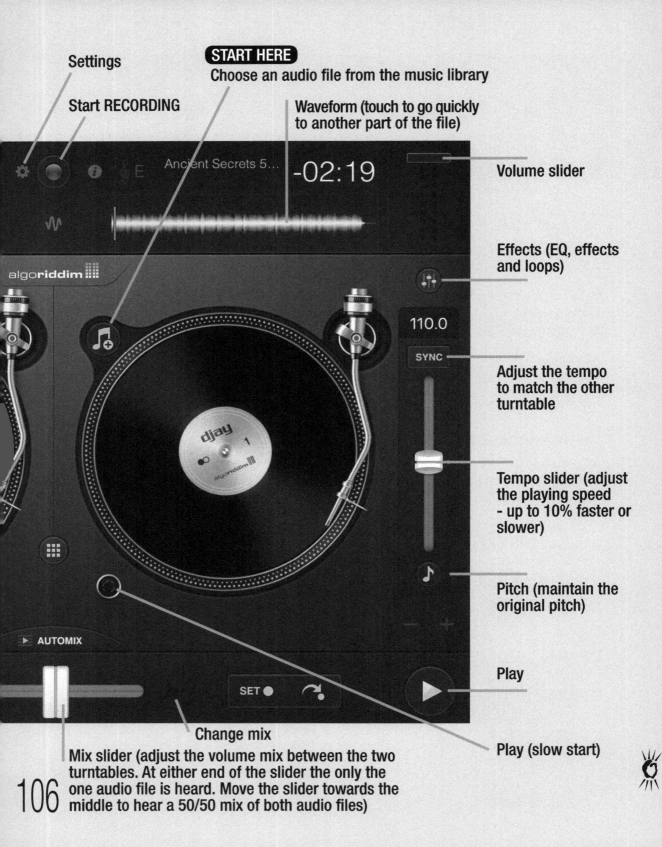

Settings

Start RECORDING

START HERE
Choose an audio file from the music library

Waveform (touch to go quickly to another part of the file)

Ancient Secrets 5...   -02:19

algo**riddim**

110.0

SYNC

djay   1

AUTOMIX

SET ●

Volume slider

Effects (EQ, effects and loops)

Adjust the tempo to match the other turntable

Tempo slider (adjust the playing speed - up to 10% faster or slower)

Pitch (maintain the original pitch)

Play

Play (slow start)

Change mix

Mix slider (adjust the volume mix between the two turntables. At either end of the slider the only the one audio file is heard. Move the slider towards the middle to hear a 50/50 mix of both audio files)

106

Recording a soundtrack

If you want to make adjustments to a single audio file, hold the iPad vertically as you only need to use one turntable. If you need to combine more than one audio file hold the iPad horizontally. **Using a playlist in the Music app will make it easier to find the music and sounds you want quickly when mixing a soundtrack.**

Preparing to mix audio files

- Load first audio file into turntable one

- Load second audio file into turntable two

- Listen to each track and if necessary adjust the volumes so they are at similar levels

- Tap Sync to adjust the speed of the files (BPM) so they will fit together better

- Depending on your djaying skills, you may want to practise putting the soundtrack together. However, there is no harm recording each practice, just in case you get it right first time. Note the timer when you want to change to the other turntable

- Make sure both files are at the start – drag the needle to the outer edge of each turntable.

Mixing example

- Tap the red Record button

Listen to djay mix from two songs and one sound effect:
www.ipadanimation.net/epub_media2.html

Listen to the above audio file as you read these instructions:

- Tap Start New Audio Recording – *recording starts immediately*
- Tap Play (slow start) on turntable one (mysterious music). The audio file starts playing slowly and speeds up, over a couple of seconds, to the final play speed
- At 28 seconds on turntable one, tap mix arrow to change (with a three second shuffle transition) to turntable two (upbeat music). If the BPM of the two audio files match the result should be a smooth transition
- Load the sound effect audio file into turntable one. Using a playlist will help locate the next file quickly
- At 12 seconds (on turntable two), quickly drag the mix slider back to turntable one and at the same time tap play on turntable one (door slam sound effect)
- Stop recording.

Choosing music

- Respect copyright (see *Copyright* on page 29)
- Music with the same beat (BPM) mixes best. Choose songs, with the same beat, or sync the BPMs in djay
- Avoid songs with lyrics as they are hard to cut mid-sentence. You'll end up waiting for the end of the verse, producing a much longer soundtrack than you want
- Use transition effects to 'hide' the music change and emphasise a new scene
- Advanced DJs choose music which has a similar harmonic sound, ie the key the music is in.

Tempo and pitch

It is a common phenomenon that increasing the tempo (making a sound faster) makes the pitch higher, eg sounding like a chipmunk. Slowing the tempo makes the pitch deeper, eg like a growling monster. Adjust the tempo slider to achieve both results. The default range for tempo adjustment is +/- 10 percent. This can be changed up to +/- 75 percent in the iPad Settings for djay (General panel – Speed Slider Range).

But one really amazing feature in djay is the option to preserve the pitch.

Now you can play a one minute song in 50 seconds (or 80 seconds) and it will sound like the original – just faster or slower.

Transferring djay recording to iStopMotion

From djay, the audio recording can be uploaded into iStopMotion's Audio Library (use the same steps to add the djay soundtrack to iMovie):

- Tap the red Record button
- Tap the name of the recording you want to use for your stop motion (the most recent recording is at the top of the list with a default name of the date and time)

- Tap the default name and type your own name

- Tap Share...
- Tap Open in...

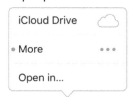

- Tap Copy to iStopMotion (or iMovie).

iStopMotion is opened and the recording is saved into iStopMotion's Audio Library.

Transfer djay soundtrack to GarageBand

- Connect the iPad to a computer
- In iTunes, select the iPad device
- Select the Apps tab
- Scroll to the File Sharing section at the bottom of the Apps window and select djay in the list of Apps
- Save the djay document to the desktop
- Either add the files into the iTunes music library, or as a GarageBand Document (see *Transferring a song* on page 97).

Characters, props and backgrounds

Creating an animation world in a set

In this chapter we cover a range of topics which relate to the set and equipment:

- Mediums for stop motion
- Backgrounds
- Cameras and lens attachments
- Remote camera
- Camera mounts
- Rigs for moving camera and set
- Picture composition
- Lighting.

Things you can use to make stop motion

Many things can be used for stop motion animation (in order of popularity):

- LEGO® (eg The LEGO Movie) – you can build a whole world at the same scale. However, the small size can make it harder to get close up pictures
- Plasticine® 3D (eg Wallace and Grommit)
- Plasticine 2D
- Whiteboard
- People
- Coloured paper
- Food
- Miscellaneous objects – pots, shadows etc.

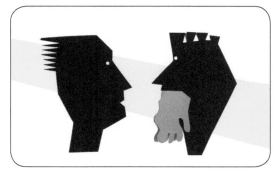

If your stop motion has a story, it is probably easier for the audience to relate to characters. Add eyes and a mouth to almost anything (such as fruit or kitchen pots) and turn them into characters.

Try to limit yourself to two or three characters. Remember that every character will need to be animated so the more characters, the longer it will take to create the movie.

Backgrounds

Backgrounds help people believe that the movie takes place where you say it does. Every part of the camera view needs to be filled with the background.

Backgrounds don't need to be detailed or accurate. They can be as simple as smudged patches of colour. You could use a collage or fabric; anything that covers the desk and wall in the room you are working in.

Every part of the camera view needs to be filled with a background. They help people believe that the movie takes place where you say it does.

Backgrounds don't need to be detailed or accurate. They can be as simple as smudged patches of colour. You could use a collage or fabric; anything that covers the desk and wall of the room you are working in.

Artwork for the base and background can be painted on large sheets of cardboard. Or use an extra large sheet of cardboard and curve it to provide the base and background. This avoids visible joins between sheets and helps create a natural horizon.

You could also make a three dimensional set with props such as buildings and furniture, or a deep jungle.

You might need different backgrounds for different parts of the story, eg a room in a house, a sports field or outer space.

Create buildings with removable walls. Create different size models of buildings – a small one for an outside shot and a much larger wall for the internal shorts.

Use tape to secure the background, LEGO bases and large props to the table so they can't move. Duct tape is strong yet can be torn by hand and is easy to remove afterwards.

Store LEGO characters in a separate smaller container, so the minifigure faces don't get scratched.

Cameras

iStopMotion usually creates clips that are 1280 x 720 (known as HD 720p). When using a device with a higher resolution camera (3rd gen iPad or later, iPhone 4 or later and iPod Touch 5G or later), you can record pictures with a higher resolution of 1920 x 1080 (known as HD 1080p). To change the recording resolution, tap the Info button in the Gallery. The higher resolution will create larger files and increase the time required to save pictures.

In general, use 720p mode unless you require very high quality and have addressed quality across all other areas of production such as story, set design and lighting.

Choose camera

Tap the Camera button at the top right to choose the back camera.

Tap Settings:

- If the picture is too light or too dark, tap Exposure in the top left and drag the circle graphic to a different part of the picture to adjust the brightness
- Most recent iPad models activate the Focus control (also in the top left). Drag the square graphic onto the part of the picture you want in focus, usually the speaking character's face.

Tap Done in the top right.

Every time you move the camera position or angle, come back to this screen and adjust the exposure and focus controls.

iPad

Modern iPads have a rear camera which can record pictures up to 1080p mode.
The iPad 2 rear camera resolution is 1280 x 720 (0.92 megapixel). This is the same resolution iStopMotion uses in 720p mode.

Remote camera

iStopMotion allows an iPhone, iPod Touch or second iPad to be used as a remote camera wirelessly connected to the main iPad. You need to be able to connect both devices to the same WiFi network.

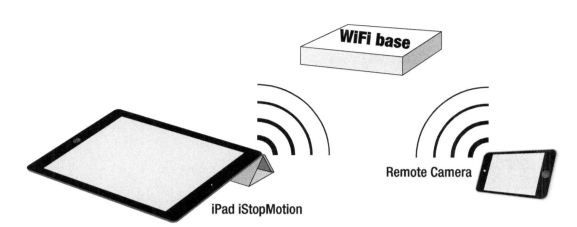

WiFi base

Remote Camera

iPad iStopMotion

All recent models of iPhone and iPod Touch suitable as a remote camera. The remote camera device will need iStopCamera from the App Store.

The advantages of a remote camera include:

- The camera does not need to be touched when recording, so won't be accidentally moved

- The iPhone and iPod Touch are smaller devices and can fit into small or awkward spaces, such as next to a bird's nest, high up on a pole or down next to an insect on the floor

- You can place the camera close to situations such as a mouse feeding or insect trail, and then step back to record the pictures without disturbing the creatures

- Devices such as the iPhone, may record better quality pictures.

The iPod Touch may be useful when you need an economical device with a small size.

The iPhone has generally has better camera specifications and records better pictures than the iPad. iPhone cameras have better camera optics, low light operation, fast aperture, low noise image compression, manual focus and macro close up.

Learn how to get the best photos from the iPhone with a guide such as *www.imore.com*

Remember to use the camera in a horizontal position for stop motion pictures. You may need to turn off orientation lock.

It takes slightly longer to save the picture wirelessly back to the iPad.

To set up a remote camera:

- Open iStopCamera on the remote camera (iPod Touch, iPhone or second iPad)

- Open iStopMotion on iPad

- Tap the Camera button in the Information Bar

- Select the remote camera from those available, in this case 'Amy's Phone'

- On the remote camera tap 'Accept' to confirm connection

- Set camera exposure, white balance and focus point, if available. The iPad shares the same screen as the remote camera, so these settings can be adjusted on either the iPad or remote camera.

When you are ready to record pictures, use the controls on the main iPad – don't touch the remote camera at all. The battery charge of the remote camera is displayed on the iPad so you can keep an eye on the battery level without touching the remote camera.

Tethering

A remote camera can also be used with a personal WiFi hotspot using an iPhone (4, 4S or later) or an iPad (3G iPad 2 or later). This service may not be available for all data plans. Some carriers may charge for data.

- iPhone (connected to a cellular network) can create a WiFi network using a personal hotspot and an iPad connects to it

- iPad (logged in to cellular network) can create a WiFi network using a personal hotspot and an iPhone/iPod Touch connects to it.

Camera lens attachments

The iPad, iPod Touch and iPhone are smart consumer devices with a camera. They are not primarily photographic devices so they don't offer a wide range of camera options.

To increase the range of pictures they can record use a lens attachment, such as:

- Folding magnifier glass – place a magnifying glass in front of the camera lens (see *Lens attachment* on page 123)
- Olloclip (iPad and iPhone).

Olloclip

The Olloclip (*www.olloclip.com*) is a one piece unit which has several lens attachments to extend the iPad and iPhone cameras.

Use the **Wide-Angle** lens when you need extra width in your picture – approximately double that of the normal iPad or iPhone. A wide angle lens means you don't have to be so far away from the subject to fit everything into the screen.

The **Macro** lens increases by a factor of ten so you can see small things magnified. It allows you to focus within 12-15mm of the subject. Watch out for shadows from the camera when you get too close.

The **Fisheye** lens captures approximately a 180 degree field-of-view. It produces some striking images for special effects by wrapping a whole 180° scene into the picture. Horizon lines will bend.

How to focus

Use camera focus to improve the clarity of the picture and to draw your eye to the part that is in focus.

In general, you want the talking character clear and in focus and the background distant and blurry.

Focus determines the distance from the camera that items will be in focus. Every object this distance from the camera will be in focus. Objects closer to the camera or further away than the focus point will be blurry.

Manual focus

Some cameras (3rd gen iPad or later) and remote cameras (3rd gen iPad or later and the iPhone) allow you to set a manual focus point. This means you choose which part of the picture is in focus and the rest of the picture will be more blurry. This is called **'depth of field'**.

Use manual focus to:

- Help your character stand out in a busy set
- Guide the audience to the part of the picture you want them to look at
- Improve your stop motion to look more like the movies we see in theatres
- Purposely record blurry pictures for titles etc.

To set a manual focus point:

- In the Clip Editor, tap the centre of the screen and on the Information Bar tap the Camera button
- Tap the camera you are using

Manual focus

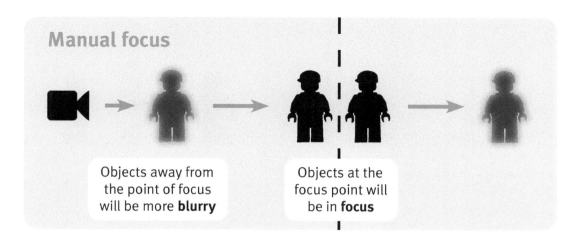

Objects away from the point of focus will be more **blurry**

Objects at the focus point will be in **focus**

- Tap Settings
- Tap the Focus button
- Tap the part of the picture you want crisp and clear – *the focus icon moves to that part of the picture.*

To get the best result from the focus:

- **Place the talking character close to the camera**
- **Increase the distance between the talking character and other characters/props**
- **Don't place important characters against the background.**

Fixed focus

Some cameras (iPad 2 and iPod Touch up to 4G) have a **fixed focus** which means that most objects will be in focus, regardless of their distance from the camera.

The main limitations of fixed focus are:

- They can't focus on objects very close to the lens. The focus range starts around 20-30cms from the camera
- You can't choose which objects are in focus and which are not.

If the object/character is very close to the lens, it may not be in focus.

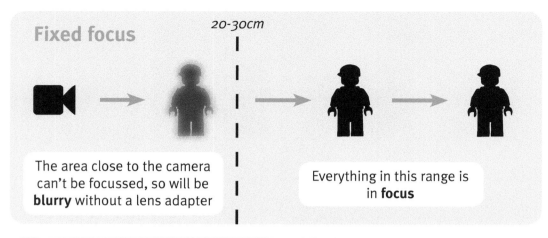

Fixed focus

20-30cm

The area close to the camera can't be focussed, so will be **blurry** without a lens adapter

Everything in this range is in **focus**

Moving the camera away will eventually bring the object/character into focus, but everything will also become much smaller.

Lens attachment

Adding a lens attachment or magnifying glass in front of the camera (particularly older devices with fixed focus) can increase the optical functionality of the camera lens. This will help to get a sharp focus on an object that is very small or very close to the camera.

In the following picture we've used a magnifying glass (such as a loupe used by stamp and coin collectors) over the camera lens which produces a crisp close-up of the small LEGO character.

The magnifier is held in position with a rubber band.

Different magnifiers will produce different results. The one we used has a focus point about 5cm in front of the lens which allows LEGO figures to fill the screen.

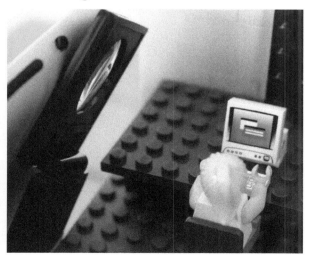

Camera mounts

Having the camera in the right position will help you record the best stop motion pictures.

Usually the camera needs to be mounted in a secure stand so that it doesn't move. There are many specialised stands available for the iPad, iPhone and iPod Touch or you can make your own.

At the other times, the camera view needs to move. Use whatever apparatus (rig) you can to move the set or camera, eg large sheet of cardboard, box, kitchen chopping board, skateboard, pull along toy etc. It doesn't matter what you use as long as the movement is smooth and the pictures have good composition.

To create the illusion that the characters are alive and moving, it is essential that the characters move but the set and camera do not.

Secure the iPad to a stand and use tape to secure the camera stand to the table. Don't use tape on the devices as they generate heat and the tape may fail.

There are two main ways to hold the camera – with a vertical stand or a horizontal stand.

Vertical camera stand

You'll need a work area on a table for your set and a wall or portable stage to support the background. Hold the iPad vertically in a stand. We've developed an iPad animation stand for stop motion work. It supports the iPad in a range of vertical and upright angles. For more information go to *www.ipadanimation.net/store.html*.

Stabile Coil

The **Stabile Coil PRO** (*www.thoughtout.biz*) is a sturdy stand for the iPad. It features a still flexible coil that can be manipulated to support an iPad camera on almost any surface and at almost any angle. This stand can support the iPad up to 45cm off the ground. The top of the coil has a pivoting cradle to hold the iPad.

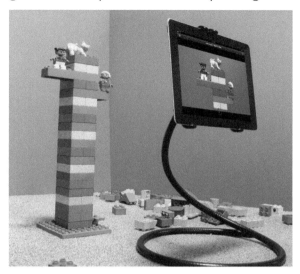

If your angles are more extreme, even upside down, make sure you also get the Grapple Pro attachment to clamp the top of the iPad into the cradle, so it can't fall.

Homemade wooden stand

You can make an iPad stand out of wood, or other solid material. The stand in the following picture holds the iPad steady and is suitable for a range of angles.

Download the plans

Download a copy of the plans to make your own iPad stand (*www.ipadanimation.net/downloads/IPA_Stand.pdf*)

Horizontal camera stand

When your stage is 2 dimensional (such as sand pictures, colour paper, 2D cutout Plasticine) lay your background on a table. Use a higher object such as a box or cabinet. Lay the camera flat on an overhanging board.

Camera stands for small remote cameras

The **Viewbase** (*www.theinyourface.com*) is a compact and secure mount for the iPhone and iPod Touch. It clamps onto any firm support, horizontal, vertical or at an angle, up to 50mm wide. Clip it on the edge of the table or hang it from an overhead rail. It is small enough to mount off a wall fitting in a tight corner and is easy to work around on your stage.

It has a flexible neck and a swivel head which can place the camera right into the set at a wide range of positions.

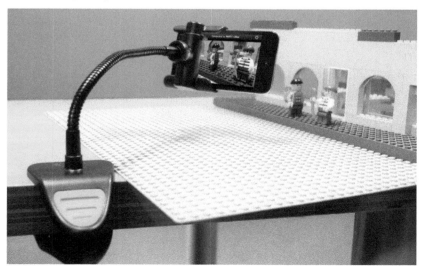

The **Ped4 Coil** (*www.thoughtout.biz*) is a smaller version of the Stabile Coil. It is a sturdy stand for the iPhone and iPod Touch. The stand is very flexible and can position the camera on any surface. It has a swivel head to position the camera at almost any angle.

Use LEGO bricks to build a support for the iPhone or iPod Touch or iPad Mini right into the set. Test the view with the lens at the top and the bottom of the device. Larger cameras, such as the iPad are heavier and less suitable for this type of stand unless you use more bricks to make the camera stable.

You can make a cardboard stand for iPod Touch and iPhone using **Achim's DIY Origami**. Go to *www.boinx.com/istopmotion/ipad/accessories* to download the template.

127

Rigs for a moving camera

In movies and on TV, we see a wide range of camera movements which are used to help tell the story. They use expensive equipment called 'rigs' to move the camera smoothly.

Add sophistication to a scene with intentional and smooth camera movements in stop motion. This can be a movie making style or used as a special effect.

Moving the camera by hand might seem an easy solution, but it usually produces a poor result. The camera needs to be very steady and the movements equal and smooth. **It might take longer to set up a rig but the result will be worth it.**

To make it easier to move the iPad stand smoothly (push, slide, rotate etc.) place it on a solid platform such as a wooden board.

Time lapse mode is often useful because you don't need to tap the record button for each picture in that scene.

Pan

– horizontal rotation of the camera

Put a pin or rod into the bottom board and make a slightly larger hole in the top board to fit over the pin. This will allow the top board to rotate. You will get a different result if the camera lens is over the pivot point, or off to one side. Use powder between the boards if they don't slide easily.

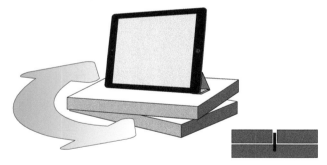

Zoom

– movement towards or away from the object using the camera lens and the angle of view.

Technically, this can't be done with the iPad, iPod Touch or iPhone, but a similar effect can be achieved by sliding the camera towards or away from the object.

Dolly

– an apparatus designed to move the camera in a specific way – up, down, along, through, over etc.

Use a solid surface such as a table, the floor or a plank. Lay a ruler or long stick across the table against the edge of the camera stand. Secure the stick to the table with tape. Slide the camera stand along the stick a few millimetres after every picture. Make sure movements are smooth and even.

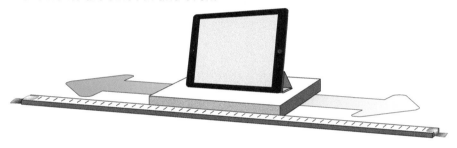

Crane (ramp)

– an apparatus designed to raise or lower the camera as it moves so it simulates flying.

This is a variation of the dolly technique. Use a solid surface such as a board on an angle. Secure a ruler or strip of wood to the board as a guide to slide the platform against and to measure equal movements.

Use almost any apparatus to make a rig to move the camera the way you want.
Use ingenuity and creativity. What can you do with a skateboard or a wheeled toy?

String can be used to enable circular movements. Ensure the string attached to the anchor point is tight to produce a smooth movement.

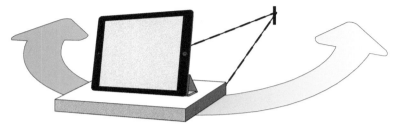

Losmandy StarLapse

Initially designed for astronomers, the StarLapse adds dynamics to time lapse stop motion with an automated camera motion. The camera can be set to pan or tilt at different speeds from 7.5° to 240° per hour to provide a smooth camera motion at any frame rate.

For more information, search "starlapse" on *www.losmundy.com*

Camera stabiliser

If your stop motion is about a journey (a trip in a vehicle, a tour around school, a treasure hunt etc) iStopMotion on the iPad is ideal because it is only one piece of equipment. It may seem easy to simply walk around with the iPad but the result may not be very smooth. A stabiliser will make the difference between an average movie and a really great one.

A stabiliser is a mobile rig for a camera which:

- makes it much easier to keep the camera level
- gives more consistency between pictures
- is more secure than holding the iPad directly
- removes the risk of accidentally pressing the Stop button.

The following picture shows an iPad in a simple homemade stabiliser mount. It has two wide handlebars and an elastic tie.

Watch the result of using a stabiliser:
www.ipadanimation.net/epub_media1.html

Download the plans

Download a copy of the plans to make your own iPad stabiliser (*www.ipadanimation. net/downloads/IPA_Stabiliser.pdf*)

Camera stabiliser and rig

For a variation of the stabiliser, attach part of the set:

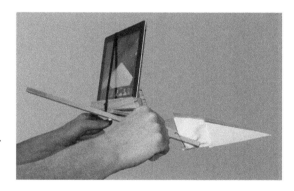

- Add a forward protruding support arm to the base of the stabiliser mount

- Secure an object, in this case a paper dart, to the support arm so it is in camera view. The camera and object are now 'one'

- Set the focus on the part you want in focus (dart or background)

- Use Time lapse to record a sequence of pictures.

If you move only between pictures and stand still while the picture is recorded, the result will be crisp, focussed pictures as you'd normally expect in stop motion (see first picture over the page).

For a different effect, keep moving as the pictures are recorded. The foreground object will remain in focus and the background will be blurry (see second picture). Yet when the movie plays the action looks fluid and real.

For the best result, move slowly in straight lines and broad sweeping curves. Experiment with time lapse intervals and your speed of movement to achieve the right effect. To add interest and visual pace, vary your speed and from time to time come to a stop.

Sometimes the effect you want can best be achieved by moving or rotating the set instead of the camera. For the best result make sure you have smooth, even movements.

Simulate an aerial 'fly-over' by rotating the set

- Do a test and make sure the camera view doesn't run out of background or that your hands don't get in the way
- Use time lapse mode for the smoothest result – use a short interval and rotate the set slowly
- If you want to rotate to a specific end point, or rotate around a certain element, use a rig to ensure the same result every time.

Rotating the set

Place a small LEGO brick with a stem in the centre of a LEGO base plate as pivot point. Around the outside of the base plate add thin smooth-top bricks to support the set base. Tape this base plate to the table.

Using a second LEGO base plate, create the actual set. Add a handle off to one side.

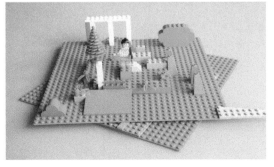

Secure the camera in position for the desired picture composition. Check that any object, visible to the camera, is part of the set. For example, to rotate a set 120° in three seconds with a playback frame rate of 12 FPS will require 36 pictures. Rotate the set a few millimetres between pictures or use time lapse with a short interval to help achieve a smooth result.

Watch a set rotation:
www.ipadanimation.net/epub_media1.html

Sliding the set

Create a long narrow set, such as a street, using several joining LEGO road base plates. Add elements along both sides of the road edge such as shop fronts, sculptures, trees, traffic lights, signs, other vehicles and characters

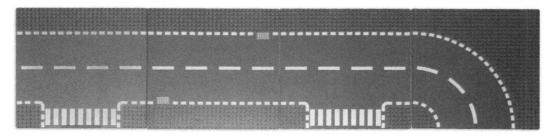

Place the camera at one end of the long side of the set and at the right height (note the spacers under the stand). Place a neutral sky background in the distance to block the camera view of anything beyond the set.

Tape a ruler to the table to slide the base against. Place a LEGO brick along the edge of the base as a marker so it is easy to measure equal movements.

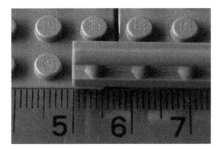

For example, sliding a set 300mm in five seconds with a playback frame rate of 12 FPS will require 60 pictures. Use the marker along the ruler edge to measure 5mm between pictures or use time lapse with a short interval to help achieve a smooth result.

How to film a moving car

Car chases are often an action highlight in a stop motion. Here is an effective way to animate a car driving. Use the set described above:

- Set the camera focus on the vehicle
- For each picture, slide the set a few millimetres past the camera (or move the camera past the set). Use the Overlay to move the main vehicle back into the same alignment with the previous picture. Animate the interactions with other vehicles and characters. Use a small piece of cotton wool to draw attention to skidding wheels.

The result will look like the camera is travelling alongside a moving character or vehicle. Add interest to the scene by changing the camera position to a view inside the vehicle or an approaching vehicle, then back to the side on view.

Another interesting camera angle is to attach the camera to the vehicle giving a view from the moving vehicle.

How to fly a rocket

Give the impression of a huge set (outer space) on a small table with this technique:

- Place a sky background on a table
- On the background place a flying craft such as a rocket or plane
- Place other items in the sky such as clouds (use cotton wool)
- Mount the camera overhead looking down on the set
- For each picture move the clouds past the craft, but don't move the flying craft.

Picture composition

The arrangement of the objects in the picture is called 'composition'. **Everything in the picture should help to tell the story.**

The following steps are a useful approach for composing a picture:

- Decide the **background** for the scene and place the camera. The background is often a fixed size so doing this first will ensure the background fills the screen
- Place the **main object** and check that any **movement** in the scene can be made within the camera view.
- Usually the main object is the **talking character**. Place them close to the camera with their eyes near a grid line (see *Rule of Thirds* on opposite page). This is a good time to set the **camera focus** on their eyes. For most dialogue scenes, the camera height should be level with the talking character's eyes, unless you are showing a specific perspective
- Place the **props** (buildings, furniture, vehicles etc)
- Place **other characters**. Remember that each character needs to be animated, so don't add more characters than you need. **A strong picture composition may also be a simple one.** Most scenes may only require one or two characters, with the occasional 'big' scene with many characters. If the other characters are important to the scene, place them close to the talking character so they are in focus, otherwise place them away from the talking character so they are not in focus.

Make a final check of the picture composition:

- Are the main objects proportionally balanced within the picture area? (see *Rule of Thirds* on opposite page)
- Are there any distracting objects?
- Does the picture have good lighting? Are shadows or reflections a distraction? (see *Lighting* on page 139).

One of the strategies for an engaging movie is to **use the camera as if it were a character. At the start of every scene move the camera to a very different angle and position to show what is happening in that scene.**

Check the exposure every time you move the camera to a new position or angle.

Rule of Thirds

The 'Rule of Thirds' is a photographic rule which helps to achieve a well balanced composition.

Grid lines (see *Clip Settings* on page 152) are thin lines marking the screen into thirds – horizontally and vertically. If you arrange main objects and shapes in your picture with one of these grid lines, your picture will have basic composition balance.

When your stop motion involves people or characters, **position the camera at the height of the character's head so the eyes are around one third down the screen**. This will go a long way towards achieving good composition.

It is a good idea to leave the grid lines on as they are not saved in the clip.

Perspective

Perspective is the way the camera views the character. You might choose different perspectives for different types of story.

Zoom

When you put the camera on a stand and get on with animating, you often produce a 'fly-on-the-wall (bird's eye)' perspective. The audience does not get engaged in the story as the character is always at a distance. This is a valid perspective when you want to show the character lost in a big situation.

Use close up views to engage the audience so they can understand what is happening in each scene and have empathy for the plight of the character.

Distant

Close-up

Height

One particular challenge with small characters (eg LEGO and Plasticine) is to avoid looking down on every scene as if a giant is looking down. If you want to show the character is scared, shy, intimidated or small, it may be appropriate to raise the camera slightly to look down at them.

Most commonly, the **camera should be at the same height as the character's eyes**. This may require raising the set, or the just characters in the scene. Add extra blocks to raise the character, as long as they are out of view of the camera.

At times you may want to look up at a character, eg if they are stuck up a tree. This may require raising the prop and character much higher than the camera.

If you want to show the character is feeling confident and bold, lower the camera slightly (or raise the character) to look up at them.

Camera higher

Eye level

Camera lower

Lighting

Most cameras work best when there is good light. With stop motion you need to **maintain the same amount of light – same brightness, intensity and colour – for every picture.**

Natural lighting from the sun

If the lighting conditions are too bright, colours have more contrast – lighter areas tend to go white and darker areas tend to go black.

In some cases, such as a time lapse of an outdoor event, strong lighting contrast and changeable lighting conditions may be an important part of capturing the real event.

Where possible, record the pictures with softer and less direct light. In the shade, on cloudy days and inside, colour contrasts are not so extreme and there is much less shadow.

139

Consistent lighting

The light from the sun changes because it is moving across the sky. The atmosphere filters the light and clouds move to block the sun. Even when you are recording inside, try to minimise the effect of the sun. Use a sheet to cover the windows or use a large piece of cardboard to shield your set from direct sun.

Consistent lighting means that regardless of the time of day or the weather, you can record pictures with the same lighting conditions. Always complete recording all the pictures for a scene before taking a break to minimise lighting changes during a scene.

Note the position of lights in the room and place your set under them to get the best light.

Also note the position of windows and make sure your shadow doesn't fall on the set.

Don't aim the camera towards a window as the brightness of the light streaming from outside will make your set too dark. You may also get reflections on your set.

For the best consistent lighting block out all sunlight and use only artificial lights.

Artificial light

Experiment with the right amount of light for your particular project. You probably won't need a lot of light – perhaps several small lights from different angles so the lighting is even and there are no shadows on your set. Use a diffuser, dimmer or a different wattage bulb to get the right level of lighting.

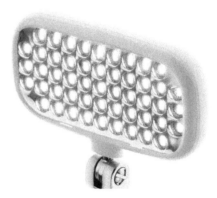

Small panels of dimmable LED lights are an economical and safe solution.

Secondhand light

A quick, cheap and safe way to add light to your set is to reuse the light you've already got. In the first picture on the next page, the characters are well lit from the right, while the left side of the picture is darker and the characters are in shadow.

In the second picture, a small piece of white paper has been added to the set to 'bounce' some of the main light onto the left side of the characters. The paper would usually be out of sight of the camera, but is shown here to demonstrate the effect.

Camera exposure

The iPad, iPhone and iPod Touch cameras automatically adjust a number of photographic settings such as shutter speed and ISO to help produce the best photo. **If you have good lighting conditions you can expect automatic controls to do a good job.**

The setting for **exposure (the relative brightness of the picture)** can be adjusted. Check the exposure every time you move the camera to a new position or angle.

- Tap the centre of the screen and on the Information Bar, tap the camera icon

- Tap Settings for the current camera. Drag the exposure dial to the part of the picture you want to use as the middle level of brightness. Areas of the picture which are darker or lighter are adjusted to suit.

Move the exposure icon over different parts of the picture to test the results. In the examples below, tapping the exposure icon on the character's light coloured hair adjusts all the colours to make them darker. Tap the exposure icon on the dark area of the desk which lightens all the colours, causing some parts to go completely white and lose detail.

Tap the exposure icon over a part of the picture which represents good middle brightness – the grey floor in this case . This produces both dark shadows and light highlights. The overall result is a good exposure setting for this picture.

If your picture composition only has dark colours, eg a night scene or in a tunnel, there may not be any part of the set which has 'middle' brightness. Temporarily place a brighter object in front of the camera and use this to set the exposure. Tap the button in the top left to 'Fixed' to keep the exposure at this level.

Likewise, if the picture only has light colours, eg a snow scene, there may not be any part of the set which has 'middle' brightness. Temporarily place a darker coloured object in front of the camera to set the exposure. Tap the button in the top left to 'Fixed' to keep the exposure at this level.

Fixed versus continuous exposure

- **Fixed exposure** – keeps the picture brightness at the same level regardless of changes to the light conditions, eg if the sun goes behind a cloud. This will help to maintain consistent lighting with less flickering between the pictures. Use this option when the pictures feature a significant foreground character or an object needs the same colouring regardless of changes in lighting conditions

- **Continuous exposure** – adjusts the picture brightness according to the lighting conditions. This is useful in situations when you want the lighting in the picture to change, eg if you are recording a time lapse in sunshine, then go into shadow, the picture will be brightened to compensate. Use this option when the pictures are of a whole scene or background. However, a character who has good colour in sunshine will suddenly become very bright as the whole picture is brightened when in shadow.

White balance

White balance compensates for a colour cast in the picture. It is often used to fix the problem that white objects do not look 'white'. Some light bulbs cast a yellowish colour over the set. Other lights cast a bluish colour.

White balance can also be used as an artistic feature, eg making a fireside scene yellowish, or a scene in a laboratory bluish.

To set the white balance:

- Tap White Balance in the header
- Temporarily place a sheet of white card in front of the camera: white card to restore balance to white, or coloured card to create a colour cast (see *Colour wheel* below)
- Tap to Unlocked to make the colour of this card the new 'white'
- Tap to Locked to store this new 'white'
- Remove the sheet to see the new colour scheme.

Colour wheel

White balance follows the principles of the colour wheel. Using yellow card, the new 'white' essentially removes yellow from the pictures making them more purple – the opposite colour on the wheel. Using purple card will make the pictures more yellow, and so on.

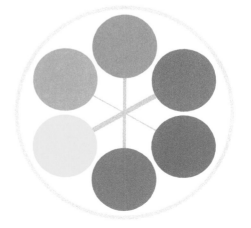

Principles of animation

These principles, developed by Disney animators in the early 1930s, help to create believable characters. The animators figured out how to make things look alive, and make characters look like they are thinking and reacting rather than just moving around like robots.

1) Squash and stretch

Squashing and stretching exaggerates object deformations. For example, when a ball bounces on the floor, it squashes flat. When an object squashes and stretches, it must maintain the same mass, but just changes shape. Plasticine squashes really well; LEGO does not.

2) Anticipation

Anticipation guides the audience's eyes to where the action is about to occur. One of the biggest problems in beginners' movies is that it can be hard to tell what's going on because characters do things suddenly for no apparent reason. For example, if a character is walking and suddenly something is in their hands, the viewer will probably be surprised because there was no indication of the impending action.

Draw attention to the action that's about to happen through anticipation. Have the character look at the thing, and then bend to pick it up.

3) Follow-through

Follow-through occurs after an action. For example, after throwing a ball, the character's hand won't just stop, it will continue moving as it returns back to a normal position.

Follow-through actions include the reactions of the character after an action, eg leap for joy, shrug of shoulders, and usually lets the audience know how the character feels about what has just happened.

4) Arcs

Everything in nature tends to move in arcs or curves rather than perfectly straight lines. Using arcs to animate the movements of characters helps achieve a natural look. Movements in straight lines make a character appear robotic or sinister.

Gravity also makes things move in arcs. If you throw something, it will curve up toward its high point and then curve down towards the ground.

5) Slow-in and slow-out

Most things have a tendency to start and stop moving gradually. For example, if a character is going to run, they won't start at full speed and then stop instantly. They should build up speed gradually and then slow down gradually.

Adapted from http://en.wikipedia.org/wiki/12_basic_principles_of_animation and www.stopmotionanimation.com

6) Timing

Timing adds emotion and intention to a character's actions. both in:

- Physical timing: the actual motions and time required to perform an action
- Theatrical timing: the pauses and emphases that make an action dramatic.

7) Secondary action

Secondary actions are little movements that aren't essential but help to add meaning to an action.

For example, if a character licks his lips as he picks up an apple it shows he expects the apple to be juicy and is anticipating the taste.

8) Exaggeration

Exaggeration is a good way to add emphasis to certain movements and draw attention where you want it. A lot of exaggeration can be achieved with *Squash and stretch*.

If your movie is about something realistic, keep exaggeration to a minimum, but if it is a comedy – use exaggeration liberally.

An action can be further exaggerated with accompanying sound effects.

9) Staging

Staging is the art of using camera angle, camera movement, lighting, composition, placement of characters and props to direct the viewer's eye. Staging means composing your shots so that the action is clear and the viewer can easily tell what's going on.

10) Solid modelling

Animated shapes need to have a clear shape and solid appearance to come to life. Solid modelling helps to convey the weight, depth and balance of the character. Plasticine and LEGO have a solid appearance and work well for stop motion. Other mediums such as whiteboard can have characters with solid shapes, whereas stick figures appear flimsy.

11) Appeal

Character personality or appeal helps the emotional connection between character and audience. Characters must be well developed, have an interesting personality, and a clear set of desires or needs that drive their behaviour and actions.

An audience wants to know that they can relate to characters in a story and that it is worth their time watching the movie.

Lastly, no one wants a bad movie review. Emphasising these tips will help you to avoid one!

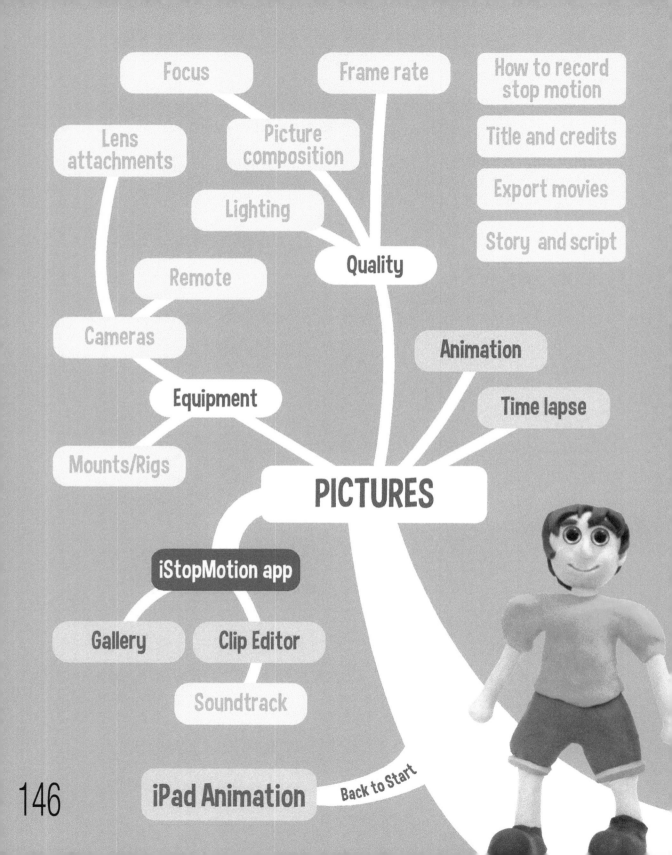

Focus

Frame rate

How to record stop motion

Lens attachments

Picture composition

Title and credits

Export movies

Lighting

Story and script

Quality

Remote

Animation

Cameras

Time lapse

Equipment

PICTURES

Mounts/Rigs

iStopMotion app

Gallery

Clip Editor

Soundtrack

146

iPad Animation

Back to Start

Create the illusion of movement - one picture at a time

Recording video clips with iStopMotion

Recording video clips with iStopMotion

We will record pictures to match the soundtrack in **iStopMotion**.

How to record stop motion

Shorter and simpler stop motion projects can be made entirely in one iStopMotion clip (see *Process 1* on page 6 and *Process 2* on page 8). Larger and more complex projects may use iStopMotion to create clips of stop motion content which can be edited into a movie later (see *Process 3* on page 9).

Step 1: Opening iStopMotion

Step 2: Soundtrack

See *Adding a soundtrack* on page 156.

Step 3: Recording pictures

See *Recording pictures* on page 167.

Step 4: Exporting clip

See *Exporting clips from iStopMotion* on page 178.

Boinx forum

If you want to connect with other users of iStopMotion, ask technical questions, or get support, check out the Boinx forum. *https://boinx. com/connect/forum*

Watch a stop motion about posting a letter:
www.ipadanimation.net/epub_media1.html

Working as a group

If you are working with another person, assign roles for each scene to encourage communication: **animator** (moves the characters and visualises the story) or **director** (operates the iPad). Swap roles regularly.

Open iStopMotion

iStopMotion has two main screens:

Gallery – stop motion clips made in iStopMotion are stored in the Gallery. The Gallery has buttons to create a new clip, edit an existing clip and export a clip for use in other apps.

Clip Editor – controls and features for recording a stop motion clip.

Gallery

Open iStopMotion. If it doesn't open in the Gallery, tap the centre of the screen and tap the Gallery button in the top left.

In the Gallery, each clip has a large thumbnail with a name, designated *'iStopMotion Clip X'* until you rename it. It also shows the date it was created and its duration (time and number of frames). If you want to change the thumbnail of the clip, tap the clip to open it, select a different picture in the Timeline, then tap the Gallery button to close the clip.

It is a good habit to rename clips to avoid confusion. Tap on the name and type the name you want.

As you start making stop motion movies, swipe your finger left or right to look through the clips made in iStopMotion.

The buttons in the Gallery include:

New – (top left) starts a new stop motion clip.

Share – options for exporting the clip (see *Exporting clips from iStopMotion* on page 178). Until you share a clip, it can only be viewed in iStopMotion. The original stop motion clip remains in the Gallery until it is deleted.

Delete – from time to time you will need to delete a clip from iStopMotion to free up space on your iPad. If you want to keep a copy, make sure you have shared a copy before deleting it.

Settings (top right) lets you set a number of features such as turning the app sounds on or off, choosing the picture size (720p or 1080p), settings for Dropbox and providing feedback on iStopMotion.

Clip Editor

The Clip Editor screen is displayed when you tap on a clip thumbnail or tap the New button.

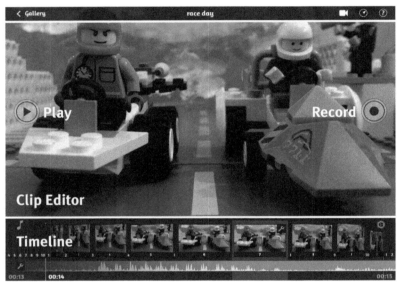

Across the top of the screen is the Information Bar. The centre of the screen is a large preview window with two large buttons and across the bottom is the Timeline.

On the left side is the Play button and on the right is the Record button.

Information Bar

Touch the centre of the screen at any time to show the Information Bar across the top of the screen. It automatically hides after a few seconds.

The Information Bar has these buttons:

Gallery – (top left) goes to the Gallery, like a 'back' button.

Camera – choose the camera you want to use to record pictures.

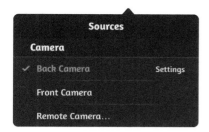

iStopMotion can use these cameras:

- The iPad's **back camera** is the best quality iPad camera and the one you'll use most often (see *Cameras* on page 116)

- The iPad's **front camera**

- A **remote camera** from another iPad, iPhone or iPod Touch running **iStopCamera** (see *Remote camera* on page 116). Other types of cameras can't be used with iStopMotion.

The Settings button allows you to set the brightness of the picture (see *Camera exposure* on page 141). You can also set the focus on some devices (see *How to focus* on page 120).

Time lapse – turns on time lapse mode and sets the recording interval between pictures. The icon changes to blue as a reminder that time lapse is selected (see *Time lapse* on page 169).

Play button

Plays the recorded pictures at the speed defined in Clip Settings.

If the movie does not play, hold the Play button for two seconds. iStopMotion will re-create the playback movie and will show a message 'Rendering Playback Movie...'.

Record button

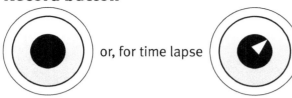 or, for time lapse

Tap the Record button to capture a picture. Hold the button to add a black or white frame. When time lapse mode is selected the centre of the button changes to show a timer, and the button starts/stops the time lapse sequence.

If the Record button is unresponsive, it may be because the iPad memory is full. Delete unwanted content from the iPad, including clips from the iStopMotion Gallery, before you record more pictures.

Timeline

Across the bottom of the screen is the Timeline which displays thumbnails of the recorded pictures.

The Timeline can only show a small range of pictures from the clip. To see an overall view of the entire clip, turn on the Navigator in Clip Settings (see *Navigator* on page 155).

The total recorded time and number of frames are stated after the last picture.

Clip Settings

The Clip Settings button, at the right of the Timeline, displays options for recording and playback.

Show

The 'Show' options, at the top, determine what you see on the screen – the last recorded picture, the camera view or a combination of both:

- The **left button** turns off the camera and shows only the recorded pictures. This is helpful when reviewing the pictures you have recorded

- **Use the middle button when animating** as it shows a combination of the camera view and the last recorded picture.

Most parts of the picture will line up exactly but the animated part, where the two pictures are different, appears as a ghosted image, clearly showing which objects have moved and which have not. In most cases, you want the character moving, while the rest of the set (objects and background) stays still

Touch and hold the centre of the screen to adjust the transparency between the two images.

The **right button** shows only the camera view. This is helpful when setting the camera for a new position at the start of each scene (see *Picture composition* on page 136).

Speed (frames/sec)

The 'Speed' setting determines how quickly the pictures play. Changing the speed will change the length of the clip. Tap '+' or '–' to change the speed between 1 and 30 pictures per second (see *Frame rate* on page 160):

- 300 pictures at 12 frames per second (FPS) will play for 25 seconds
- 300 pictures at 30 FPS will play for 10 seconds.

If your pictures have been recorded to match the soundtrack, the speed must be set before the pictures are recorded as if it is changed later they will be out of alignment.

Sometimes with time lapse, the clip speed can be adjusted until it 'feels' right. Tap the Play button and then tap on the Clip Settings to change the speed of the clip as it plays.

Grid lines

Tap the Settings button in the lower right and turn on Grid Lines.

Grid lines divide the screen horizontally into three equal areas and vertically into three equal areas. Use these guides to help arrange the picture composition (see *Rule of Thirds* on page 137). Aim to have key elements, such as horizon line, the edge of a building or the eyes of the talking character, near one of these grid lines for photographic balance.

Grid lines are only seen on the screen and are not saved to the clip. Generally, it is useful to leave the grid lines on.

Navigating the clip

To navigate around your clip, either:

- Tap the Navigator, if displayed above the Timeline, to go directly to a different part of the clip

- Tap a thumbnail in the Timeline to display that picture

- Swipe, left or right, across the thumbnails to scroll through the clip

- Swipe two fingers across the Timeline, to jump to the beginning or end of the clip.

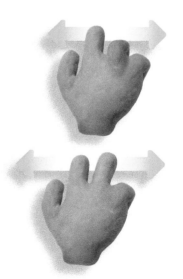

Navigator

The Navigator is useful for navigating through longer clips. When selected in Clip Settings, the Navigator appears above the Timeline and shows a compressed view of the entire clip...

...or the soundtrack, whichever is longer.

Actions

The Actions button, in the top right of the current thumbnail, accesses editing tasks such as delete or duplicate pictures. Duplicated pictures are added after the original. This is useful as an editing task to slow down a sequence either for effect or to align the pictures to the soundtrack.

Delete All will completely erase the stop motion and is followed by a confirmation. Reverse Order is useful for actions are that best recorded in reverse. Sometimes these sequences need to be recorded in their own clip and then added to the movie project in iMovie.

Delete Frame

Delete All 317 Frames

Duplicate Frame

Reverse Order of 317 Frames

155

Adding a Soundtrack

The movies we see on TV and in the cinema rely strongly on sound to add power to the pictures. It is important that you make the best effort to have a high quality soundtrack because **ears process sounds more quickly than eyes**.

Respect copyright when you use someone else's music (see *Copyright* on page 29).

There are two steps to add audio to a clip in iStopMotion:

- Import the audio file to iStopMotion Audio Library. In some cases you may record audio directly in iStopMotion using the iPad microphone
- Select and add the required audio to the picture clip.

Importing audio files to iStopMotion

The soundtrack needs to be complete in one file. If the soundtrack has several audio files combine them together in GarageBand or djay.

There are a number of ways to add a soundtrack to iStopMotion. They all involve importing the audio file into iStopMotion's Audio Library. All audio in the Audio Library is available to all iStopMotion projects.

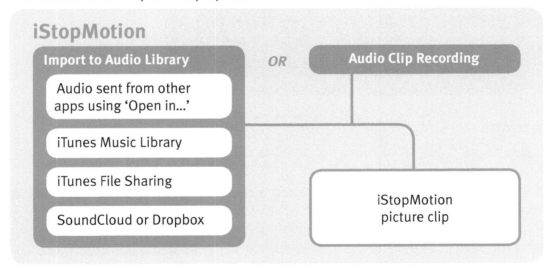

Directly from another app

Some apps, such as GarageBand and djay allow you to send audio directly to the Audio Library in iStopMotion using the Share option – 'Open in…'.

iTunes music library

Import audio from the music library on your iPad to the Audio Library in iStopMotion.

Via iTunes File Sharing

Refer to *Transferring music from a computer to the iPad* on page 102, except change all references of GarageBand to iStopMotion.

SoundCloud

SoundCloud is a web based service for sharing and storing audio files. Upload the audio to SoundCloud from any device then download directly into iStopMotion.

Dropbox

If you have a Dropbox account, upload audio files to it from a wide range of devices and download them directly into the Audio Library in iStopMotion.

Adding a soundtrack to a stop motion clip

In iStopMotion's Clip Editor:

- Tap the Audio button

- Tap **Audio Library** to see a list of audio files stored in the iStopMotion Audio Library

- If the audio doesn't appear in the list and is available in the iPad's Music Library, SoundCloud or Dropbox, tap one of the Import buttons
- Tap the **triangle** to the right of the name and listen to a preview of that audio
- Tap the **name** of the audio file and it will be added to the clip.

Recording audio directly in iStopMotion

Simple sound requirements can be recorded directly into iStopMotion using the iPad microphone (see *Recording with a microphone* on page 44). You can connect an external microphone to the iPad to improve the quality of the recording.

These 'clip recordings' are not part of the Audio Library and are only available for the current stop motion clip.

Clip recordings are suitable for simpler requirements such as narration. If you want to combine music, sounds and narration you'll need to play the music and make the sounds in the room and talk on top of them. Do a test recording to get the balance right and then record them all together in one take.

In most situations, you'll need to use GarageBand to create the best sound mix.

In iStopMotion's Clip Editor:

- Tap the Audio button

- Tap **Record**

- If you want to limit the length of the audio recording to the duration of the pictures in the clip, tap the waveform button next to Record

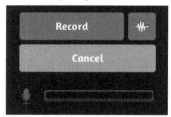

- Tap the red Record button
- Wait for the three second countdown and record your audio
- Tap Stop when you've finished

- Tap Use, and it will be added to the stop motion clip.

Audio options

When a clip has a soundtrack, a blue band appears along the bottom of the Timeline showing the waveform.

Tap the Audio Options button at the left end of the band.

Offset changes the start of the soundtrack:

- **A negative offset** (eg -6 frames) **will cut off the start of the sound** – this may be useful when you want to skip the first part of the sound, or for a larger project (see *Process 3* on page 10) to record a particular scene

- **A positive offset** (eg 14 frames) **adds silence** before the start of the audio.

The fade sliders gradually increase or decrease the volume at the start or end of the soundtrack. Fade Out is particularly useful where the clip is shorter than the soundtrack and you don't want the soundtrack to end abruptly.

Working with audio files

If you want to change the soundtrack in iStopMotion, the current one must be removed first:

- Tap the Audio button

- Tap Remove Audio. The audio file remains in the Audio Library

- Tap the Audio button again and select another soundtrack.

To delete an audio file or clip recording from the Audio Library so it is no longer stored in iStopMotion:

- Tap the Edit button in the top left of the Audio Library

- Tap the red circle icon next to the audio you want to delete

- Tap the Delete button to confirm

- Tap Done in the top left

- Tap Cancel to return to the Clip Editor.

159

Frame rate

The frame rate is the number of pictures that play every second in a clip, ie frames per second or FPS. Frame rate is one factor which determines how smooth or jumpy your stop motion animation will be.

It is possible to start recording pictures for your stop motion without any planning. For example, if you only record 72 pictures you may have problems turning them into a movie. In this case, the realistic outcome may be a movie that runs for only six seconds (72 images / 12 frames per second = six seconds). Therefore it is best to set the frame rate before you start recording pictures.

Frame rates for animation

In Clip Settings, choose a frame rate (play speed) between 1 and 30 frames per second. For animation, the frame rate needs to be decided at the start so you record the right number of pictures to match the soundtrack.

Choosing the right frame rate for your stop motion is a balance between time and quality. The number of pictures directly determines how long it takes to record them. Choose fewer frames per second and you'll finish your stop motion more quickly. If the frame rate is too low it will affect the smooth quality of the animation.

Watch examples of different frame rates:
www.ipadanimation.net/epub_media1.html

The frame rate can be changed after the pictures are recorded. This may be useful with time lapse. However, don't change the frame rate if the pictures match the soundtrack.

The following frame rates will be the most useful for stop motion animation:

1-6 FPS

Very low frame rates are suitable when you have a short time to record the stop motion or the subject matter suits a more jumpy result. At 1 FPS, a one minute stop motion will have just 60 pictures.

These low frame rates work well for:

- slideshows (1 FPS). Duplicate the picture to achieve a frame rate longer than one second
- animated artistic works using graphic mediums such as painting and sculpture (2-6 FPS)

- stories told with media such as paper cutout characters (6 FPS)
- a first practice stop motion, or where you don't have much time.

10, 12 or 15 FPS – 'half speed'

The eye perceives smooth motion above 10 frames per second producing good animation results. Use this for most situations.

These frame rates are half the full speed frame rates, which we will look at next.

These 'half speed' frame rates are an economical way to achieve good animation in a reasonable time. They are suitable for almost any situation where realistic animation movements are required, including stories using LEGO or Plasticine characters.

At 12 FPS, a one minute stop motion will have 720 pictures.

25 or 30 FPS – 'full speed'

If you want to make stop motion for TV or movie theatre, choose 25 frames per second (or in North America choose 30 frames per second). The worldwide standard for high definition television (HDTV) uses 30 frames per second, so this may be the best choice. iMovie uses 30 FPS.

These high frame rates can produce very high quality animation as long as all other areas of production, such as lighting, set design and story are also high quality.

At 30 FPS, every minute of stop motion will have 1800 pictures.

How do frame rates affect animation time?

Choosing a higher frame rate does not increase the animation time by the same ratio. For example, increasing the frame rate from 6 to 12 (or 15 to 30) doubles the number of pictures, but does not increase the time for story development, recording the soundtrack, making props or arranging the picture composition. **Doubling the frame rate may only increase the total production time by 20 percent.**

How do frame rates affect character movements?

Regardless of the frame rate, characters should move at a realistic speed. For example, if you want a character or object to move across the screen in four seconds:

- One FPS will mean large movements (eg 5cm) between pictures. The character may appear to jump in only four pictures

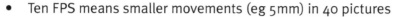

- Ten FPS means smaller movements (eg 5mm) in 40 pictures

- Thirty FPS means very small movements (eg 2mm). You'll need a steady hand for these very small and delicate movements. You will also need a lot more time to record 120 pictures.

It can be helpful to act the action, eg walking across the room, to help decide how long the action should take, and therefore, how many pictures are required.

Frame rates for time lapse

As time lapse sequences are recorded automatically, there is no difference in the effort to record enough pictures to playback at 1 FPS or 30 FPS – just choose the appropriate time lapse interval. If you can, record enough pictures for full speed, ie 25 or 30 FPS.

It is best to estimate how many pictures you need before you start (see *Time lapse* on page 169).

The speed can be changed later (between 1 and 30 FPS) so that the clip matches the 'feel' of the soundtrack and, hopefully, the length of the soundtrack. For example, a time lapse of a sunrise at 20 FPS might look rushed and feel disconnected from the soundtrack, whereas at 17 FPS it might better fit the pace and therefore 'look' smoother as well.

Frame rates in iMovie

iMovie only works at 30 FPS. Any iStopMotion clip edited in iMovie will be converted to 30 FPS regardless of the original frame rate. iMovie does a good job of duplicating frames so the result is usually acceptable. If you want the best quality for your stop motion movies, avoid editing your stop motion clips in iMovie, or record them with a frame rate that multiplies evenly to make 30, eg 1, 2, 3, 5, 6, 10 or 15 FPS.

Recording pictures

There are two ways to record stop motion pictures:

- **Manual animation.** Lightly tap the Record button to record one picture. Move the character and repeat. Caution: tap the Record button on the iPad very gently so you don't accidentally move the camera as this could ruin your clip.
  Manual animation is more suitable when you have lots of characters or need to make a different number of animation movements every time.

- **Time lapse.** This is an automatic mode that records pictures without the need to touch the iPad. It is like an extra pair of hands that record the pictures automatically for you, see *Time lapse* on page 169.
  Time lapse is useful when you have a simple repeat movement. Time lapse also helps you to finish the scene more quickly.

Use whichever recording method you prefer and switch between methods as often as you like.

See the *Animation process* diagram on page 166.

At the start of each scene:

- Listen to the next part of the soundtrack and decide the required movements, eg character talks for 3 seconds then walks to the door. In the *'My Story'* project we advise listening to the whole soundtrack and noting when each scene starts in order to reduce unnecessarily handling of the iPad during animation

- Tap the Settings button and tap the right 'Show' button

- Decide how that part of the story should 'look' and arrange the characters and props

- Move the camera to a very different angle (move more than 30°) or magnification to show what is happening in the scene. One of the strategies for an engaging movie is to use the camera as if it were a character in the scene. Make sure the background completely fills the screen.

  At times you may need to change the placement of objects on the set to record the perspective you want, eg temporarily remove the wall of a building

- Arrange the characters and objects. **Ensure the talking character is clearly obvious**. If the character is too small move them closer to the camera, or if they are too low stand the character on extra blocks out of view of the camera.

  Vary the camera view between wide angle (showing the whole scene) and close ups

163

- Decide where the character will move during the scene and make sure the movement can be seen by the camera
- Decide whether manual animation or time lapse is suitable for the scene
- **Set the focus** (if your camera has focus control) on the part of the picture which best helps to tell that part of the story, usually the talking character
- **Check that the overall picture composition is simple, clear and interesting**
- Tap the Settings button, tap the centre 'Show' button and you're ready to animate the next scene.

Opening scene

The first pictures you record need to get people interested in the story. Choose a picture composition which is simple and suitable for the title.

The opening scene may be a simple movement such as a car driving by, or a view of the background. Don't start animating the story, and in most cases don't show the characters, until the start of the first sentence.

Title

The first pictures you record need to get people interested in the story. Choose a picture composition which is simple and suitable for the title. We'll add the title onto the pictures later in iMovie although sometimes you may want to animate it and this needs to be done first.

Land of Secrets

How to animate

Tap the Record button on the right side of the screen then move the character or object a small amount, eg 5mm or 10mm. Remember that you'll need to record 6, 15, or even up to 30, pictures for every second of movie, so plan your movements accordingly.

For the best result, it is essential that you don't bump the camera as this may move the picture alignment (see below). Also, take care you don't bump the table or the set. Use Duct tape to secure things that should not move.

Repeat the cycle of moving characters and objects then recording a picture until the end of the scene. Attempt to record the whole scene before handling the iPad or reviewing your progress or if you need to take a break. Use the end of an action or movement to 'hide' a change in lighting or accidental camera movement. After you have recorded all the pictures for a scene, take a break to watch your movie so far.

If you need to delete a 'mistake' picture, eg a hand in shot, tap the Actions button on that picture and select 'Delete frame'.

If you need more pictures to bring a particular action into alignment with the sound, tap the Actions button on a picture before that point and select 'Duplicate frame'.

If you need to insert a sequence of new pictures, record them in a new iStopMotion project and edit them together in iMovie.

Keep it simple

Three characters are often enough to tell a story. Each additional character increases the overall animation time. Increase the scale of your stop motion by choosing one scene to use a larger number of characters.

To reduce the risk of moving the iPad:

Avoid moving the iPad in a scene, Here are some ways to reduce the risk of bumping the iPad:

- Use Time Lapse

- Use the volume button on Apple branded headphones to record a picture

- Use a remote control such as the Satechi Bluetooth Multi-Media Remote (*www.satechi.net/index.php/ bluetooth/bluetooth-remote*). Press the play/pause button to record a picture

- Use a Flic button (*http://flic.io*)

- Use a remote camera (see *Remote camera* on page 118).

Animation process

Recording pictures is a simple task with two parts:

- animate (move) the character, and
- record the picture.

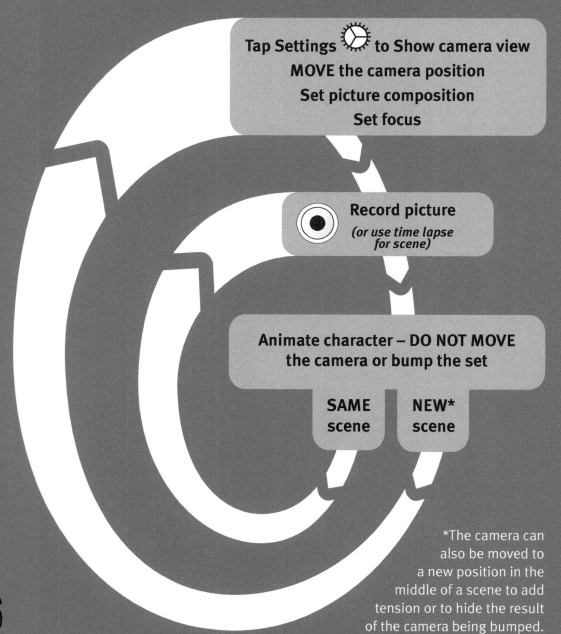

Tap Settings to Show camera view
MOVE the camera position
Set picture composition
Set focus

Record picture
(or use time lapse for scene)

Animate character – DO NOT MOVE the camera or bump the set

SAME scene

NEW* scene

*The camera can also be moved to a new position in the middle of a scene to add tension or to hide the result of the camera being bumped.

166

Animating characters

A common goal of stop motion is to give life to inanimate objects. When telling a story, you want the audience to believe the character is alive.

We expect the character to move and the set to remain steady, so take care to secure the set and camera with duct tape.

Characters convey their personality by the nature of their movements, eg weary, energetic or crazy. Download instructions for LEGO minifigure walk from *www.ipadanimation.net/store.html.*

These are some basic tips for character movement:

- Movements in curves are better than straight lines

- Change speed gradually

- Use small movements before a big action, eg getting ready to jump, to draw attention to the big action – the jump

- Exaggerated movements will always look better than small movements

- In general, the talking character should move and other characters should either not move or only slightly move

- Use arm, head and body movements to show that a character is talking. Use big or small movements to indicate their level of enthusiasm, excitement or anger.

Plasticine characters can be moulded to show many different body and facial expressions. Sometimes it is easier to design them with interchangeable body parts to minimise deformation and prolong the look of the original body shape. Use beads for eyes as they maintain their shape and colour.

When the character is viewed from the side, turn their head slightly so some face detail is visible to the camera.

Some LEGO minifigures have an alternative face expression which can be useful to indicate when the character has a particular mood.

Three characters are often enough to tell a story. Each additional character increases the overall animation time. Increase the scale of your stop motion by choosing one 'epic' scene to use a larger number of characters.

After the last scene (Credits)

After the last picture has been recorded for the last scene there are two final image tasks:

- Record extra pictures to fill all the spaces under the soundtrack. This could be a closing story action such as the character walking or driving into the sunset. These extra pictures will allow the music to finish, and if the credits are to be added in iMovie, provide pictures over which to add the names. If you are short on time, record one picture and duplicate it to fill all the spaces.

- Add the names of the people who made the stop motion in the credits. The credits can be animated now or simply added as text in iMovie.

The animation two rules

Of all the tips for making better quality stop motion movies, these two 'rules' will make the most improvement:

Rule 1: Don't move the camera

Secure the camera in a position where there is good picture composition. Don't touch the camera again until the next scene.

Move ONLY the characters and objects between the pictures to tell the story. Don't move the backgrounds and common objects in the set. **Use duct tape to secure everything to the desk so it can't move.**

If you move the camera randomly or too often – even slightly bumping it – the background may move and your clip may be confusing and hard to watch.

Rule 2: Move the camera

From time to time, move the camera to a completely different angle to show a new picture composition which helps to tell the next part of the story.

In general, leave the camera in each position for at least one second (eg 12 pictures when the speed is 12 FPS) or until after the sentence or the end of the scene, unless you are making a stop motion with a highly graphic effect such as a music video.

Time lapse

This is an automatic mode that records pictures without the need to touch the iPad. Time lapse is a powerful way of capturing a visual record of an event and summarising it in a short time, eg a flower opening, the moon rising, a building construction, even a security camera.

Time lapse is also useful for recording specific scenes in a stop motion story. When the animation requires a repeating interaction with objects, eg adding bricks to a stack or a character driving across the screen, it can be quicker and easier to use Time Lapse mode for that scene.

Time lapse is particularly useful because you don't need to touch the iPad, avoiding the risk of bumping it.

Calculate time lapse interval

Before recording a time lapse, calculate the interval to record the correct number of pictures.

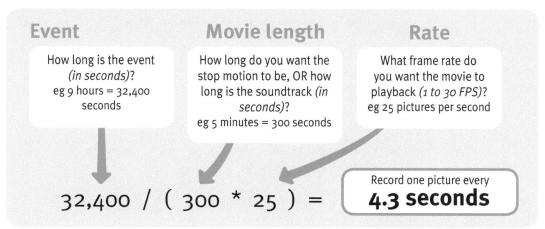

Event

How long is the event *(in seconds)*? eg 9 hours = 32,400 seconds

Movie length

How long do you want the stop motion to be, OR how long is the soundtrack *(in seconds)*? eg 5 minutes = 300 seconds

Rate

What frame rate do you want the movie to playback *(1 to 30 FPS)*? eg 25 pictures per second

$$32{,}400 \ / \ (\ 300 \ * \ 25 \ ) \ =$$

Record one picture every **4.3 seconds**

To turn on Time Lapse mode:

- Tap the centre of the screen and on the Information Bar tap the Timer button

- Tap Time Lapse mode
- Select the required interval (in seconds) between pictures.

Example: a car drives across the screen. Set time lapse to 5 seconds – enough time to move the car, withdraw your hand from the set and wait for the picture to be automatically recorded. Repeat until the car has reached the other side. If there were several vehicles on the road allow more time – 8 seconds.

When using a remote camera (second iPad, iPod Touch or iPhone), it takes slightly longer to save the picture back to the iPad, so the minimum time lapse interval is slightly longer.

When Time Lapse mode is selected, the Timer button becomes blue and the Record button displays a timer in the centre.

Using time lapse

Set the exposure to accommodate changing lighting conditions.

iStopMotion displays a countdown and can play a beep to help you get into a rhythm of: 'MOVE the object, keep CLEAR of the camera view, WAIT for the countdown and the picture to be recorded', and repeat.

If the time lapse clip is too long, try changing the play speed or delete pictures from the start or the end. If you need to delete a lot of pictures it will be easier to edit in iMovie.

Countdown

In Time Lapse mode, the Record button changes to show a countdown (of seconds) with a red progress indicator around the perimeter of the button.

Beep

iStopMotion gives an audible countdown beep up to three seconds before the next picture is recorded.

To hear the beeps, tap the Info icon in the top right of the Gallery. On the Settings panel under User Interface, tap Play Sounds on, and make sure the iPad volume is turned on.

Fixing mistakes

If you accidentally bump the camera (or the table or the set), it may move the whole scene out of alignment and ruin the clip. **Don't try to move the camera back to the same position**. Here are some ways to fix a 'bump':

- Delete the pictures for that scene and start that scene again
- Move the camera to a new angle to disguise the 'bump'. Small and random camera movements will look like mistakes, whereas a completely new angle will look like a continuous recording using multiple cameras. For a natural look, the camera angle needs to move at least 30°
- Ignore it and accept the result.

If you record a wrong picture, eg a hand in the shot, **don't try to fix it immediately as this will risk bumping the camera in the middle of the clip. Record another picture in that position**. After you have recorded the whole clip go back and delete the 'wrong' picture.

NB, in some cases, the style of stop motion, eg whiteboard illustration, deliberately shows the artist's hands drawing the pictures or arranging the objects.

Bending time

Record sequences with different time lapse intervals in the same clip. This simulates an effect where the action speeds up or slows down, eg a crawling snail starts off really slow (short interval), speeds up (longer interval), then slows down (short interval).

The technique will work for anything that moves at a constant speed, eg cars in traffic, snail sliding across a table, clouds moving across the sky.

171

Animation example: Scary Sea

Here are images of the different camera views and character actions for a stop motion called 'Scary Sea' created by Holly (9) and Emily (12).

The story was improvised using the seven question story outline. The movie is one minute long.

View the stop motion at *www.acumen.net.nz/pages/NMSScarySea.html*.

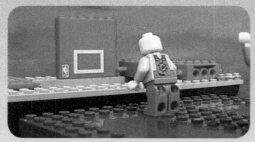

Bland image over which to add the title later.

Camera view from shore, as characters get on boat.

Camera view from boat.

Overhead camera view of whole scene.

Camera view looking up at boat.

Camera view from boat, as shark circles.

"I know karate. I will punch it in the nose"

Camera view looking up at boat.

Swimming to shark.

Sequence of random blurry images to convey action.

"The shark is dead*. We could turn it over . . . and row it to the boat!"

Camera view down in the water.

Overhead camera view of whole scene.

Safely back on boat and sail away.

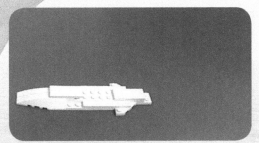

Bland image over which to add the credits later.

*We don't condone killing sharks. This was an accidental outcome of the attempt to chase the shark away.

Special effects and techniques

The term 'special effects' is a general description for a diverse range of effects, from camera and prop movements, to lightning, explosions and illusions.

The best movies always have a strong and simple story. **Special effects can increase the power of the story, but should never be better than the story.**

Special effects are completely optional; a good movie won't need them, but they are also an opportunity to do something impressive. For example:

- use cotton wool to simulate smoke, steam and mist
- flicker a torch or mobile phone light across the set to create lightning
- dangle thin strips of clear plastic in front of the camera to simulate rain
- rotate the set, use a camera movement or create a short 'epic' crowd scene with many characters.

 *Watch examples of animation special effects:* www.ipadanimation.net/epub_media1.html

Smoke

Cotton wool produces an excellent effect for smoke, steam and clouds.

Place the vehicle at the start point. Check the picture composition and focus etc, and place a marker on the stage, out of sight of the camera. Do the same for the end point.

The example used **time lapse** with a four second interval. Between pictures move the vehicle, add cotton wool (smoke coming from the tyres of a vehicle) and lift hands clear of the camera.

Rain

There are many ways to simulate rain. This is one way:

- Cut a clear plastic bag into 3mm strips
- Tape one end of each strip to the edge of a ruler
- Set the camera focus on the character
- Hold the strips close to the camera, so they are not in focus
- As you record pictures, constantly shake the ruler so the strips appear blurry.

Lighting effects

We've already discussed general lighting for stop motion. In addition, lighting can be used to create effects.

To create the effect of lightning, shine a bright light to wash out the set for one picture, then cover the set to darken it from room light. Repeat several times with reducing extremes. This is a powerful and realistic effect when it matches the soundtrack.

To create the effect of the movement of the sun, place a light on a stand a short distance away from the set. This will work best if your set has tall props nearer the front of the set. Gradually move the light to change the shadows cast on the set. The movement of shadows and glimpses of reflection from various reflective surfaces could be used to indicate the passing of time or as a break between scenes.

Use small lights such as an LED torch to put a spotlight on one character or light one part of the set. Even the light on a mobile phone can be used to boost the light on one area. Watch out for reflections on shiny surfaces such as LEGO.

Crash

When an action is very sudden, explosive, violent or physical (such as a car crash), take the audience right into the centre of the action. To show the pictures in the crash, hold the camera in your hands. Change the angle and position of the camera as if things are being thrown about in the crash. Record enough pictures for at least one second or to match the sound.

This recording process is very fast when you use time lapse, and means you don't need to actually destroy a large set. It also means you don't have to try to suspend debris in the air. Moving the camera as the pictures are recorded will make them blurry, which for this purpose is a good thing. Record more pictures than you need and delete the ones you don't need afterwards.

Use the overlay to keep part of the set in the same position in each picture.

Gunshot

Some actions require split-second timing. One of the advantages of creating the soundtrack first is that pictures can be recorded to match the sounds exactly. Use the waveform to plan the animation leading up to those time critical sounds.

In this example, the gun is raised high when the waveform shows the start of the shot and then drops back down slowly over the next few frames.

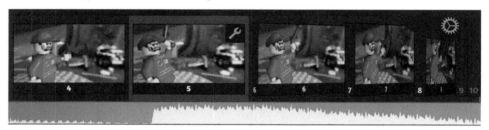

Jumping/leaping/flying

Characters often need to make movements which require a complex set up – just how do you make a character jump through the air?

Fortunately, our brain is good at filling in the gaps. If we see someone approach a horse and then ride off on it – we believe we saw them get on the horse! The actual mid-jump shots of the character suspended in the air, are not necessarily required.

Emphasise the foreground

Help the audience to follow the story by placing the characters prominently in the foreground. In this example, we've used a lens attachment so the small character can be close to the camera.

Raise the character with extra LEGO bricks (note yellow bricks under feet) so their eyes are one third down the screen (see *Rule of Thirds* on page 137).

Use extra bricks wherever you need them, as long as they are out of the camera view.

Sliders

If you need to move a character or object smoothly across a set, the effect can be achieved by securing the character to a long flat stick, such as a ruler. Secure another ruler to the set to slide the first ruler against – this will give a smooth movement. Make sure the sticks are not visible in the camera view. Raise the character up on extra bricks if necessary.

Exporting clips from iStopMotion

When you have recorded all the pictures for your clip or movie:

- From the Gallery, tap the Share button

- Tap Movie. If your stop motion has less than 200 pictures you have the option to export it as a GIF

- Tap 'Save Video' to save the movie to the Camera Roll.

Camera Roll

The Camera Roll is part of the Photos app for storing photos and video clips.

Photos and video clips, from apps such as iStopMotion and iMovie, can be saved into the Camera Roll.

When you connect your iPad to a computer, transfer the clips from the Camera Roll to the computer in the same way that you transfer photos.

WELL DONE!

You've recorded all the pictures for your stop motion

The final step may be to add the title and credits *(page 179)*

Turn clips into movie masterpieces

Making clips into a movie using iMovie

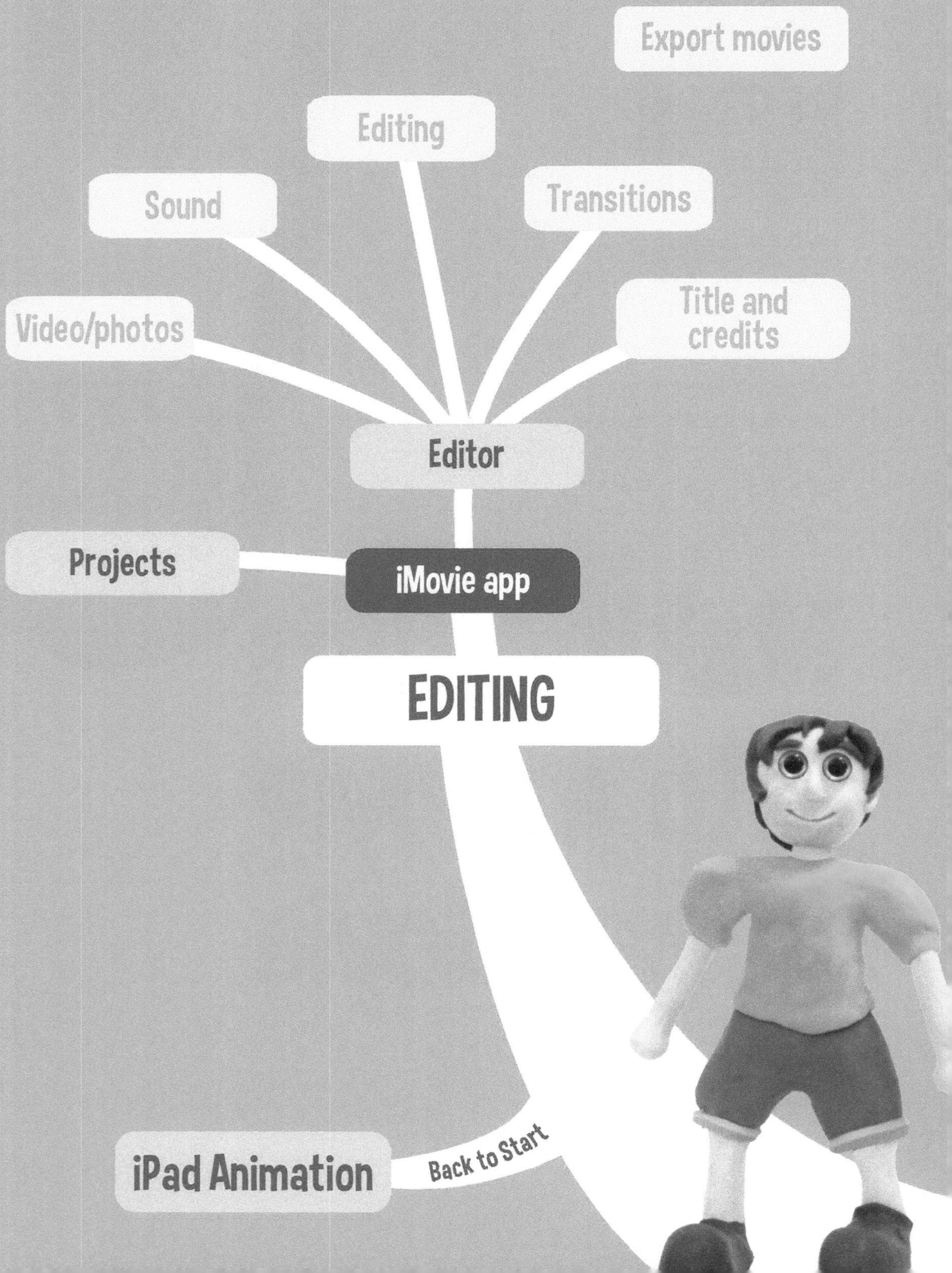

Export movies

Editing

Sound

Transitions

Video/photos

Title and credits

Editor

Projects

iMovie app

EDITING

iPad Animation

Back to Start

Making clips into a movie using iMovie

Because of the nature of stop motion animation, not every project will need editing. Each picture is only recorded when it is the one you want. So there is unlikely to be a lot of excess video content. Although, time lapse is an automated process which often records more pictures than required. The easiest way to trim surplus time lapse content is editing in iMovie.

The most common task editing task for stop motion movies is to add the title and credits in iMovie. Although, in some cases you may have even animated the title and credits.

Before you start, make sure each stop motion clip has been saved to the Camera Roll (see *Exporting clips from iStopMotion* on page 178).

Projects

Open iMovie.

The first screen is the **Projects browser** which stores all the movie projects. If you don't see the Projects browser, tap the button in the top left.

Swipe up or down to look through the movies made in iMovie. If this is your first movie skip the next page.

Tap a thumbnail picture to see information about the project.

Each movie has a thumbnail picture with a name, designated *'My Movie X'* until you rename it. It is a good habit to rename movies to avoid confusion. Tap the name and enter the movie name on the keyboard.

The length of the movie and the date the project was last changed are also shown.

Play – movie in full screen mode.

Share – options for exporting the movie. Until you share a movie, it can only be viewed in iMovie. Tap 'Save Video' to save the movie to the Camera Roll. The original movie remains in iMovie until it is deleted.

Delete – from time to time you will need to delete a movie to free up space on your iPad. Make sure you save a copy to the Camera Roll and upload it to another device before deleting it from the iPad.

Edit

To edit a movie tap Edit.

Editing a stop motion movie

Watch an edited stop motion:
www.ipadanimation.net/epub_media3.html

At first glance, this stop motion may look like a regular video recording. However, the stick insect moves very slowly, so it was recorded using time lapse with an interval of one picture per second. This sped up the movements by a factor of twelve (when the play speed is also 12 FPS).

Without time lapse, this clip would have taken the same time to record but the movie would have been twelve times longer.

To **start a new movie** (from the Projects browser):

* Tap the New Movie button in the top left

* Tap Movie

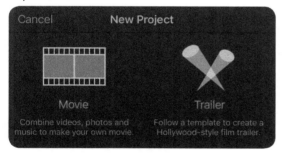

* From the Moments screen select the clip/s you want to use (you can add other clips later)
* Tap Create Movie at the bottom.

Editor

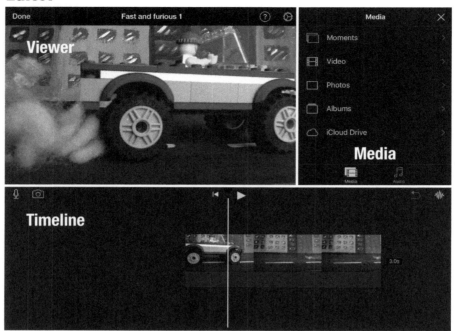

The iMovie Editor has three parts:

- **Viewer** – watch the movie here as you make it

- **Media** – access to videos, photos and audio

- **Timeline** – arrange and edit the various elements for the movie. The vertical line is the playhead. The Timeline scrolls past the playhead. Tap the Play button (in the centre of the screen) to watch the movie.

iMovie themes

At various points in iMovie, you will see options called 'Theme'.

These are built-in designs for transitions, titles and background music. Tap the Settings button (gear icon) in the top right to change the theme.

If you change the theme, all the transition, title and music options designated 'theme' in that project will change to the new theme.

Undo

If you make a mistake when editing, tap the Undo button.

Touch and hold the button to Redo.

The most common editing tasks for a simple stop motion are:

1) Adding video into the iMovie project

2) Splitting clips

3) Adding a title and credits

We'll cover these editing tasks first in this order, then cover other iMovie editing features after that.

Adding video

To add video content in addition to that already included as the 'moment':

- Tap the Media button in the Media panel

- Tap the Video button to see the video clips available on the iPad.

  In each category the videos are listed with the most recent at the top. If you don't see your stop motion clip, go back to iStopMotion and Share it to 'Save Video'

- Tap the stop motion clip you want to use – *it highlights yellow*

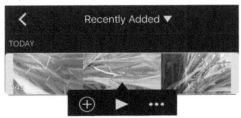

- Tap the triangle 'play' button to view the clip in the Viewer, or drag over the clip to view a particular part of it

- Slide the yellow bars at either end to shorten the clip, if necessary. Although it is more accurate to trim the clip in the Timeline

- Tap the Plus button to add the clip to the Timeline.

When the Timeline has clips, the new clip will be added at the join nearest the playhead.

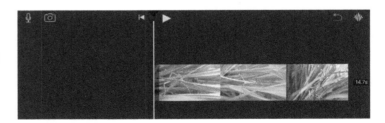

Use the pinch to zoom in or out as required when editing – *touch two fingers on the Timeline and spread them apart to zoom in, or bring them closer to zoom out.*

Navigate forward or backward with a swipe. Touch and hold on either end of the Timeline to quickly go to the start or end of the movie.

Splitting a clip

You can only add one block of text per video clip and the text is visible for the duration of the clip. Therefore, **the most common editing task will be to split the movie into smaller clips**. If you want the text on only part of the clip, such as a title at the start and the credits at the end, split the clip into smaller clips of the right length. Watch the start of your movie and decide where you want the title.

- Drag the movie left or right in the Timeline so the playhead is where you want to split the clip (for the title). Watch the Viewer as you choose the position as not every clip image is shown in the Timeline

- Tap the clip – *it highlights yellow*

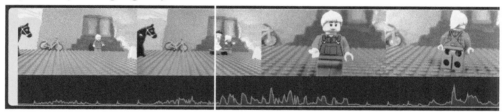

- Tap the Actions button from the bottom

- Tap Split.

The 'None' transition style between the clips will not affect audio playing smooth across the split.

Swiping your finger downward over the playhead will also perform a split. Swiping your finger upward will add into the clip a still image of the current picture for 2 seconds (freeze frame effect).

Adding a title

- Tap the clip where you want the title to appear – *it highlights yellow*
- Tap the Titles button (bottom of screen)

- Tap the style of title. The first style is determined by the Theme. If you change the theme (in Settings), the style of title automatically changes to the new theme
- Tap the screen position for the title
- Tap on the sample text in the Viewer and type your title.

The text size will automatically adjust if you have lots of words. If you want to have several displays of words, split the video clip into multiple pieces

- Tap Done to close the keyboard.

Repeat this process to split the clip and add the credits to at the end. If you don't have enough pictures for your credits, tap the camera button and record a picture to use as a still image over which to add the credits.

For more information about creating customised titles, see *Title and Credits* on page 265.

Simple stop motion movies may at this stage be complete, in which case go to *Saving the movie* on page 198. Otherwise, refer to the following pages for instruction on other editing features.

Other editing features

Deleting a clip

To delete a clip:

- Touch and hold the clip until it pops off the Timeline
- Drag it upwards until a cloud appears then lift your finger off the screen.

You can also tap the clip, then tap the delete button (in the bottom right).

Changing clip order

To change the order of a clip (it may be easier to use Pinch to zoom out):

- Touch and hold the clip until it pops off the Timeline
- Drag the clip to the new position so it plays in the right order.

Trimming a clip

If your clip has sound, tap the waveform button to view the soundtrack. This should help you to avoid trimming important sounds.

- Tap the clip – *it highlights yellow*
- Drag the yellow bars at each end to shorten the clip.

Precise editing

For more precise editing of the exact transition between clips:

- Tap the transition icon between the clips
- Tap the yellow double arrows under the transition icon – *the two clips appear in multi-track mode.*

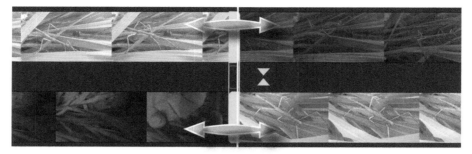

The images in the Timeline don't show every image in the clip, so watch the Viewer to choose the edit point

- In the top, clip drag the top yellow bar, left or right, to the required end point
- In the bottom clip, drag the bottom yellow bar to the required start point
- Tap the yellow double arrows to close multi-track mode.

Recording video

If your project requires additional video clips (not stop motion) or photos, which have not been saved to the Camera Roll, record them directly in iMovie. This might be useful for additional images for the credits, such as a group photo.

Make every effort to record the best quality sound you can (see *Sound versus noise* on page 40).

To record video directly into iMovie:

- Tap the Record button to activate the iPad camera

- Make sure the camera is set to video (not photo)
- Tap the Record video button
- Record the clip, then tap Stop
- Tap the Use Video button to add the video to your movie, or tap the Retake button to record it again.

Adding photos

If you want to add a photo to the movie:

- Tap the Photos button at the bottom of the Media panel
- Tap a photo add it to the Timeline at the join nearest the playhead. Photos are automatically given a duration of six seconds.

To record a photo directly in iMovie:

- Tap the Record video button to activate the iPad camera

- Make sure the camera is set to photo (not video)
- Tap the Record button
- Tap the Use Photo button to add the photo to your movie, or Retake button to record another picture.

Photos are automatically given a zoom/pan effect (known as 'Ken Burns' effect in some programs). If you want to adjust this effect:

- Tap the photo in the Timeline
- Tap the Start button in the Viewer

- Use the pinch gesture in the Viewer to adjust the zoom, and drag the photo to adjust the position, for the start view
- Tap the End button in the Viewer

- Use the pinch gesture in the Viewer to adjust the zoom, and drag the photo to adjust the position, for the end view
- Tap Done in the top left.

To remove the zoom/pan effect, set the start and end points to the same position.

To change the duration of a photo:

- Tap the photo in the Timeline
- Drag a yellow bar to the required length. **The minimum duration for any photo or video clip in iMovie is 0.3 seconds. This is only 3 pictures per second and is not a substitute for creating stop motion.** iStopMotion can display up to 30 pictures per second.

Screen capture

If you need an image from the iPad screen (any app or game), press the iPad Home button and the on/off button at the same time. The screen will flash white and save a picture of the screen to the Camera Roll. Add the screen capture to the movie in the same way as adding a photo.

Transitions

A transition is the way video clips and photos change from one to another.
A transition is automatically added between every clip.

There are a range of transition styles, as shown by their icons:

 none

 theme

 cross dissolve (not available if the clip is too short)

 slide (up, down, left or right)

 wipe (up, down, left or right)

 fade (through black or white).

To change the transition style:

- Tap the transition icon in the Timeline
- Tap the transition style, from the bottom of the screen
- If choosing slide, wipe or fade, tap the transition icon again to select the direction
- Tap the duration, eg 0.5s.

Adding sound

iMovie has five channels for sound, which comprise:

- Soundtrack of the original video or stop motion clip, if any
- Background music track (coloured green)
- Three layers for sound effects (coloured blue) or voiceovers (coloured purple).

Tap the Audio button in the Media panel.

Theme Music and Sound Effects are built-in to GarageBand. Playlists, Albums, Artists and Songs access the iPad's music library.

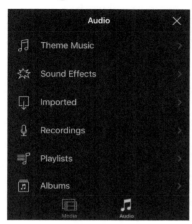

Tap the audio you want:

- Audio files **more than 60 seconds long** are added to the Timeline as **background music, in a green bar**. Background music begins at the start of the movie and, if the movie is long enough, plays completely through and loops. You can shorten the green bar and add additional background music

- Audio files **less than 60 seconds long** are treated as **sound effects** and added to the Timeline as a **blue bar**. Blue bars can be moved to any position in the Timeline

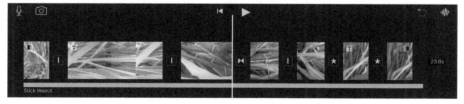

- Tap the waveform button to see the shape of the sound. This is a useful way of 'looking' at the sound when editing.

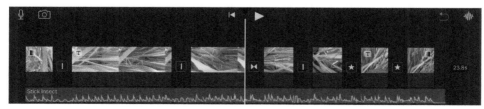

193

To edit an audio clip, tap the bar – *it highlights yellow.*

- Change the volume

- Adjust the sound level at the start or end (fade)

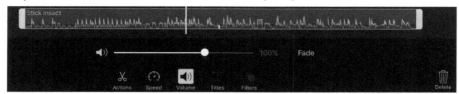

- Change the speed (tempo). Changing the speed changes the pitch.

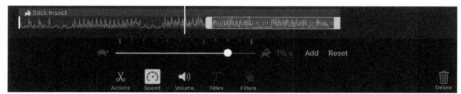

If you want to maintain the original pitch, tap off the audio clip, go to Project Settings and turn off 'Speed changes pitch'.

To change a clip shown as a blue or purple bar to background, tap the Actions button and tap 'Background'. The clip will become green.

To change a green bar to be used as a sound effect (blue bar), tap the Actions button and tap 'Foregound'. The clip will become blue.

Sound effects

Sound effects add emphasis to specific actions or story events in the movie and need to be positioned at specific points in the Timeline. Up to three sounds can play at a time.

Choose sound effects from the built-in sound effects or use one of your own from the music library. **It is a good habit to use a playlist in the Music app to store the sound effects you want to use.**

When adding sound effects (files less than 60 seconds), drag the Timeline so the playhead is where you want the sound to start.

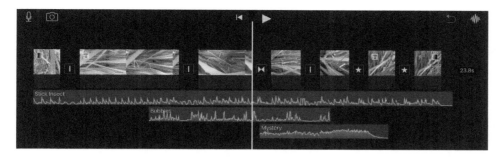

To shorten the sound effect:

- Tap the bar – *it highlights yellow*
- Slide the ends of the bar inwards to shorten it. Use the pinch gesture to adjust the Timeline scale for more accurate adjustments. Add a fade to ensure the sound starts and ends smoothly.

To move the sound effect to a new position, hold the blue bar until it pops off the Timeline, then drag it to a new position.

Getting additional sound effects and music

To create the best original soundtrack you'll want to use the most appropriate sound effects and music – go to *Getting sound effects and music* on page 34, or go to *www.stop-motion-handbook.com/pages/audio_resources.html*

Add voiceover

Make sure you know how to use a microphone (see *Recording with a microphone* on page 44).

To add a voiceover, drag the Timeline so the playhead is where you want the voiceover to start:

- Tap the Microphone button

- Tap the red Record button and wait for the three second count
- Record your voiceover as you watch the video play. The sound from the movie is muted so it doesn't affect the recording
- Tap Stop to finish your voiceover
- Tap the Review button to listen to the recording. If you made a mistake, tap the Retake button to record again, or the Cancel button
- When you are happy with the recording, tap the Accept button.

The voiceover audio clip is shown as a purple bar (see over page).

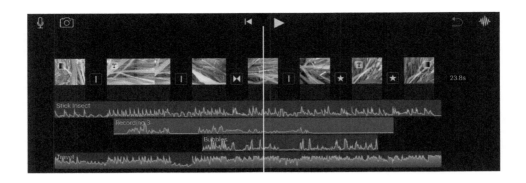

Editing a larger project

On page 10 we outlined *Process 3*, where larger stop motion projects could be recorded as separate clips, possibly by different people on different devices. If they shared parts of a common soundtrack, and the audio had been offset for the start of each clip, here is how to join all clips to the full length soundtrack.

Import all clips into the Timeline:

- Tap the Video button in the Media panel. Tap to select, then tap to add the clips you want to use

- Arrange them in order in the Timeline

- If extra pictures were recorded at the start and end of each clip these can be used for transition effects, otherwise make sure the transition style is none

- Tap the Audio button in the Media panel then add the full soundtrack to the background – *it displays in green along the bottom of the Timeline*

- If the audio waveforms are not displayed, tap the waveform button to 'see' the shape of the sound.

Use precise editing to adjust the start for point for each clip so it's waveform aligns with the full length soundtrack:

- From the start of the Timeline, tap the transition icon between clips

- Use the pinch to zoom in for accuracy

- Tap the yellow double arrows under the transition icon – *the two clips appear in multi-track mode*

- Drag the yellow bars, left or right, so the picture changes at the right place and the waveform in the bottom clip aligns with the green background waveform

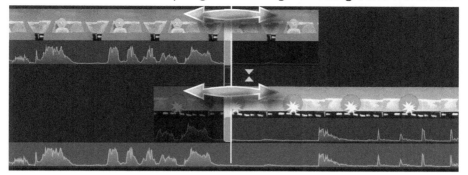

- Tap the yellow double arrows to close multi-track.

Repeat this process to align each clip to the background soundtrack.

Turn off the audio for each clip, so only the full length soundtrack plays:

- Tap each clip
- Tap the Volume button at the bottom of the screen
- Tap the speaker icon to mute the sound.

Saving the movie

When your movie is finished, tap the Done button, in the top left, to save it.

Exporting from iMovie

The movie can only be played on this iPad within iMovie. To use or access the movie in other places (eg uploading to the internet), save a copy to the Camera Roll.

On the Project screen, tap the share button.

Tap 'Save Video' to save the movie to the Camera Roll.

A resolution of 720p should give the best quality for movies comprising stop motion clips, unless you recorded the stop motion clips at the higher resolution of 1080p. Alternatively, 360p and 540p create smaller files which may be more suitable for emailing or uploading to the internet.

Even if you only want a movie with a small file size, it is a good habit to save a high resolution copy of the movie for future use.

Even if the movie has been shared, the original clips remain in the Camera Roll and the movie project remains in iMovie until it is deleted.

WELL DONE!

You've completed your stop motion

The last step may be to host a premiere
(page 200)

199

Premiere

If you've decided you want a special first screening of your movie, be sure to:

- Invite as many people as you can

- Choose the biggest screen you've got access to

- Connect some big speakers

- Shut the curtains

- Start with the speeches – thank your guests for coming, tell them about the movie and the people who made it, but don't say what happens

- Hand round the popcorn

- Turn off the lights and press play.

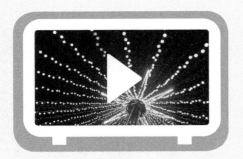

Follow us through 9 stop motion projects and learn how we did them

Stop motion projects

Stop motion projects

In this chapter we demonstrate how to make stop motion movies with these projects.

- Christmas lights
- Metamorphosis
- Race day
- Road trip
- Fly on the wall
- Sports day
- Food art
- My story
- Water cycle
- Titles and credits.

For each project we show how the pictures were recorded and how the soundtrack was created. They cover a range of topics and scenarios using time lapse and stop motion.

Using the soundtrack files (license)

The soundtrack for each project was created entirely on the iPad by songwriter Theo Corfiatis. The files are copyright and are provided (via download) **for your personal use in relation to learning about stop motion and music creation.**

They cannot be used for commercial purposes. The soundtrack files cannot be redistributed in any form to anyone else unless they are part of your own creation.

To purchase a **license to use multiple copies of the soundtracks,** such as in a classroom situation, go to *www.ipadanimation.net/store.html*.

For **additional permission to use this music for other purposes (including commercial usage),** or to have original GarageBand music composed and supplied for your project, contact Theo Corfiatis (*www.bluexrysalis. com*).

Downloading the soundtracks

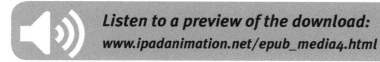

Go to *www.ipadanimation.net/index.php?page* to register your copy of iPad Animation and download the soundtrack files for the projects in this chapter.

The files need to be downloaded to a computer and then transferred to the iPad.

> ***Listen to a preview of the download:***
> *www.ipadanimation.net/epub_media4.html*

Installing MP3 files on the computer the iPad syncs to

- Add the MP3 files into iTunes on your computer
- **Create a playlist to make it easier to locate the files**
- Add the playlist to the iPad
- Click Sync and eject the iPad.

Accessing MP3 files on the iPad

The MP3 files are available in the iTunes Music Library.

Installing GarageBand files on the computer the iPad syncs to, and Installing MP3 and GarageBand files on another computer

- Open iTunes on the computer
- **PC only** – select Edit····▸Preferences and on the Devices tab deselect 'Prevent iPods, iPhones and iPads from syncing automatically'
- Connect the iPad to a computer
- Open iTunes on the computer and select the iPad device
- Select the Apps tab
- Scroll to the File Sharing area at the bottom of the Apps window and select GarageBand in the list of Apps
- At the bottom of the GarageBand Documents panel click 'Add...' and follow the prompts to add the GarageBand files (xxx.band) or the MP3 files. On a Mac you can also drag the files from the computer into the GarageBand Documents window. The files are immediately transferred to the iPad

- Click Done. **DO NOT CLICK SYNC**
- Eject the iPad.

Accessing GarageBand files on the iPad
- From the My Songs screen in GarageBand, select the Location 'On My iPad'
- Swipe one finger left or right, and up or down, to locate the song
- Tap on the song to open it.

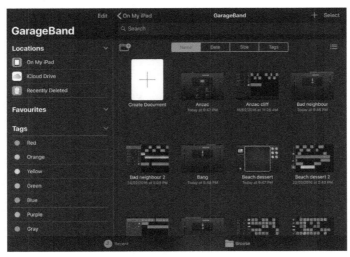

CHRISTMAS LIGHTS

Capturing the spectacle of a festive event

Time Lapse

In a downtown park, an enormous Christmas tree is set up each Festive season. It is seven storeys high and is decorated with hundreds of thousands of coloured lights which display a constantly changing light show.

The advantage of iPad iStopMotion is there is only one piece of equipment to carry and set up in a public place.

The stages of the project are:

- Recording the pictures (iStopMotion)
- Creating the soundtrack (GarageBand)
- Editing pictures and combining with soundtrack (iMovie).

Watch Christmas Lights stop motion:
www.ipadanimation.net/epub_media4.html

207

Recording the pictures

- Make sure the iPad is **fully charged** as recording may be limited by the battery charge

- Use a **secure stand** so the camera is positioned at the right angle and won't get knocked. (We used a Stabile Coil stand as it is suitable for uneven ground.)

- Turn off the sound, as a 'beep' in a public space may cause unwanted attention

- Find a camera position with a good and interesting picture composition. Check the picture won't be affected by movement of people, sun etc. For example, could someone walk in front of your camera, or park a car to block your view?

- Set the camera **exposure**. If you are recording the passing of dusk to dark, use continuous exposure to allow the lighting to change. If the sky is already dark, fixed exposure may work better

- Check the **white balance**

- Set the **time lapse** interval. In this example, the patterns in the lights were constantly changing, so we set a short interval of three seconds. At this interval it will take up to one and a half minutes to record a one second clip at 30 FPS.

  If you want a ten second clip, expect to leave the camera untouched for more than 15 minutes.

The intention was to record pictures from different angles. It doesn't matter whether all sequences are in the one iStopMotion clip or several clips. Because we'd record hundreds, even thousands, of images editing this type of stop motion will be easiest in iMovie.

From each vantage point:

- Tap the Record button to start recording

- Remain near the camera to ensure its safety and that it does not get moved. If it is bumped, the clip can be split at that point during editing to disguise it

- As the camera lens is relatively wide angle, make sure you don't get too close to the front of the camera and accidentally record yourself. If you record pictures you don't want, eg someone walks in front of the camera, don't interrupt the recording process as those pictures can be removed later

- Tap the Stop button when you've completed recording each sequence.

From some angles, such as directly underneath the tree, you won't be able to see the recording's progress on the screen. These notes may help:

- Hold the iPad directly above you to make sure the picture has good composition

- Tap the Record button to start recording

- Carefully lower the iPad down onto the stand. Make sure the screen is not sitting flat on a surface as this will put the iPad to sleep and stop the recording. The Stabile Coil stand easily adjusts for this extreme angle.

After recording

- **Review** all clips in iStopMotion. Delete individual problem pictures, such as the first few jumpy pictures, or where someone walked in front of the camera. All other editing will be easier in iMovie

- Adjust the **playback speed** (Clip Settings) so the pictures look their best. In our example, we had recorded 1740 pictures. At 12 FPS they played for a total of two minutes and 25 seconds

- **Export** each clip from iStopMotion to the Camera Roll. Choose the picture quality – in most cases this is HD/Full Size - High Quality 1280 x 720.

Creating the soundtrack

The soundtrack needs to tell the story of the pictures. Watch the clips and get a feel for the pace and mood of the activity in the pictures. In this case, the tree lights have a rhythmic pulsing pattern – regular but always changing.

We will create a GarageBand soundtrack with one loop track and two instrument tracks:

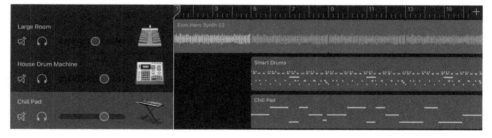

- Start a new song
- In the Instrument Browser, swipe left or right to until you see the Audio Recorder
- Tap Voice
- Tap the Tracks button

- Tap the Sections button and set Section A to 16 bars (about 36 seconds).

Track 1: Tap the Loop button and add the loop Synth loop – *Euro Hero Synth 02*.

This is an electronic sound to match the mesmerising nature of the flickering lights. The loop is four bars long. Drag it to the start of the first track and it will repeat four times within the 16 bars. Tap the microphone button and apply the *'large room'* sound effect.

The 'large room' sound effect adds big expansive echoes, like a stadium. It works best with clear single notes such as a piano, whereas repetitive sounds can mix together and become 'muddy'. However, in this case the sound has a strong repetitive beat and the 'large room' effect is used to make the sound less aggressive and more 'muddy'.

Track 2: Tap the Instrument Browser and add a Smart Drums Instrument with the *House Drum Machine* sound. Smart Drums are a fast way to get a good basic rhythm. Position the playhead at bar 5 to start the drums after one cycle of the synth loop. Tap the 'dice' button until you hear the drum rhythm you want. Tap record.

Track 3: Tap the Instrument Browser and add a Keyboard with Pad sound – *Chilli Pad*. This track is a simple one finger melody. It lifts the automated and rhythmic music in tracks one and two with something for the ear to focus on – a personalised touch. Note the two places in the music to flick the Pitch Wheel upwards at the same time as the note is played. This track also starts in the 5th bar.

Flick Pitch wheel upwards

Find the original GarageBand file and the MP3 of this soundtrack in the download.

Editing the stop motion movie

- In iMovie, open a new project and add the picture clips from the Camera Roll to the Timeline

- Save the project with a name

- In GarageBand, share the soundtrack directly to the iMovie project using 'Open in...'

- In iMovie, split the picture clips to keep the best parts. To keep the movie interesting, trim clips into pieces that are two to four seconds

- Arrange the clips in the Timeline

- Set transitions between clips (we used one second Cross dissolve)

- When the length of the clips are the same length as the soundtrack, delete the unused clips from the Timeline

- Add the title and credits

- Export the completed stop motion. Tap 'Save Video' to save the movie to the Camera Roll. Select 720p size.

Metamorphosis

Time lapse is ideal for recording events that naturally happen over several hours – such as a caterpillar forming into a chrysalis, (or a chrysalis hatching into a butterfly). These events are fascinating to watch and we can observe the whole process using time lapse.

The stages of the project are:

- Recording the pictures (iStopMotion)
- Creating the soundtrack (GarageBand)
- Combining pictures and soundtrack (iMovie).

 **Watch Metamorphosis stop motion:**
www.ipadanimation.net/epub_media4.html

Recording the pictures

This type of event often happens outside and it can be difficult to get the camera in a suitable position. Conditions such as wind and changing light also present challenges. Recording inside is more controllable and predictable.

- **Connect the iPad to power,** just in case the event takes a long time

- Choose a **background** image – a colourful painting to recreate a natural location, or plain white card to profile the chrysalis without distraction

- Arrange **lights** to brighten the picture and to even out variations in natural lighting. Make note of whether the room lights are on or off and make sure they don't get changed while you are recording. You need to leave these lights on if recording through the night

- Position the **camera** so the chrysalis is as large as possible. Put the iPad on the same base as the leaf to avoid movement between the two

- Set the camera **focus**

- Set the camera **exposure**. Fixed exposure maintains a consistent picture brightness

- Set the **white balance** to ensure vibrant and accurate colour

- Set the **time lapse** interval. This event will take place over many hours and we want to see the whole process. We chose an interval of 30 seconds

- Tap the Record button and walk away. If necessary, make sure there is a barrier so interested people can't get too close and accidentally bump the camera and ruin your clip. Also, make sure no one can stand in front of any light source, including windows in the room, as this will affect the picture colour

- Tap the Stop button when you've completed recording.

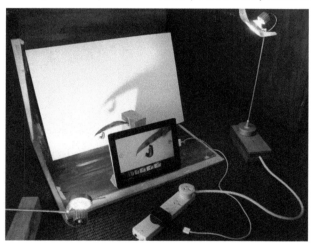

After recording

- **Review** all clips. Delete individual problem pictures, such as an insect on the set. All other editing will be easier in iMovie

- Adjust the **playback speed** (Clip Settings) so the pictures look their best. In our example, we had recorded 528 pictures over 4 hours. At 12 FPS they played for 44 seconds. The actual moment of transition from caterpillar to chrysalis is recorded in just 13 pictures (six and a half minutes in actual time – next time we'd choose a shorter interval). This was the particular detail we wanted to highlight, so the speed was determined by this scene

- **Export** the clip from iStopMotion to the Camera Roll. Choose the picture quality – in most cases this is HD/Full Size - High Quality 1280 x 720.

Creating the soundtrack

Recording the pictures first can help inspire a soundtrack. These 'cycle of life' events are very spectacular and can carry a big cinematic sound.

The caterpillar clip starts with a long lead up without much action. The soundtrack needs to build anticipation that something is about to happen – and then it happens.

Smart strings

- Start a new song

- From the Instrument Browser, swipe left or right to until you see Strings

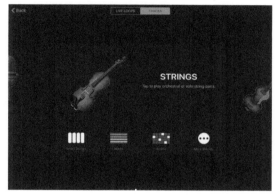

- Tap Smart Strings.

Listen to Metamorphosis soundtrack:
www.ipadanimation.net/epub_media4.html

A you listen to the soundtrack identify the three different ways to play the Smart Strings (in order – Pizzicato, Staccato and Legato):

Pizzicato	*Staccato*	*Legato*
Tap a sequence of strings to create short sharp plucking sounds.	**Tap and quick swipe** for sharply bowed sounds which have a brighter tone.	**Touch and drag** a continuous movement to create a long bowed sound. Press harder and drag more quickly to increase the intensity of the sound.
		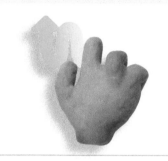

The GarageBand soundtrack has three instrument tracks.

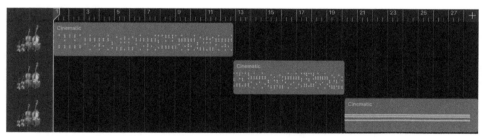

Only one clip plays at a time, so they could be played as one piece in one track. Recording the soundtrack in three parts means if you make a mistake you only need to re-record that particular part, not the whole soundtrack.

Tap Settings and increase the Tempo to 140 (beats per minute) – *this makes the notes shorter and the sound faster*

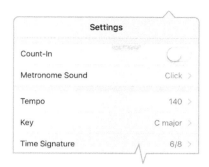

Settings

Count-In	○
Metronome Sound	Click >
Tempo	140 >
Key	C major >
Time Signature	6/8 >

Change the time signature to 6/8 to put more beats into each bar and allow the Autoplay to play faster notes

Tap the Sections button and set Section A to 28 bars (about 37 seconds).

Track 1: Tap *(Pizzicato)* the pattern indicated below – up and down the notes F, C and G. When 'End' is tapped, immediately repeat the pattern a second time at a faster speed.

Track 2: Tap and quick swipe *(Staccato)* the same pattern. Repeat a second time at a faster speed. The brighter sound builds the energy of the soundtrack.

Track 3: Complete the soundtrack with a long bowed sound *(Legato)*. Touch a finger on 'Start' and drag continuously across the screen for five seconds. Continue to drag more slowly for a further three seconds to end with a quiet sound.

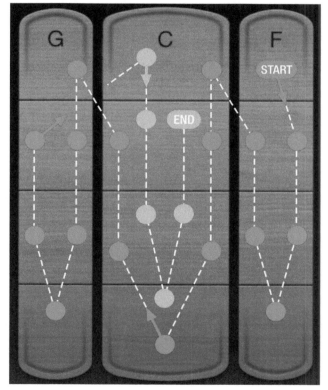

Alternative soundtrack – guitar

The second version of the soundtrack has two instrument tracks and up to four tracks recorded with the microphone.

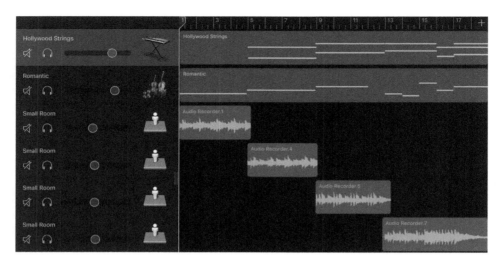

- Start a new song
- Swipe left or right to until you see Keyboard
- Tap Synth
- Tap Settings and set the Tempo to 116 (beats per minute)

- Change the Key Signature to B♭ which will slightly lower the pitch
- Change the time signature to 6/8 which puts more beats into each bar allowing the Autoplay to use quicker notes
- Tap the Sections button and set Section A to 18 bars (about 29 seconds).

Track 1: Keyboard with *Hollywood Strings* sound. The music comprises only 6 chords, each held for up to 4 bars duration.

Track 2: Smart Strings with *Romantic* sound. Set to play notes and just use the Bass. This track uses a similar melody to track 1 but adds a deeper sound. Choose the style of music instruction which suits you.

Only one track plays at a time so they could be played as one piece in one track. Recording in four parts means if you make a mistake you only need to re-record that particular part, not the whole piece.

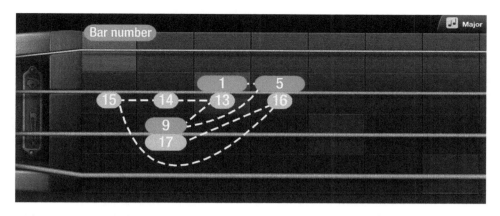

Tracks 3-6: Audio Recorder. Record a short piece of guitar picking or strumming based on the music notes of track 2. To keep in time with first two tracks, listen to them through headphones so the sound is not re-recorded though the microphone.

Hang the microphone end of the iPad off a desk and play the guitar about 30cms away (see *Using a microphone* on page 37).

For each Audio Recorder track, tap the microphone icon and apply the 'small room' sound effect. This effect adds a short echo producing a richer sound.

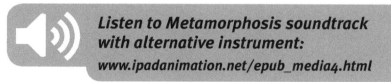

Listen to Metamorphosis soundtrack with alternative instrument:
www.ipadanimation.net/epub_media4.html

Find the original GarageBand file and the MP3 of this soundtrack in the download.

Editing the stop motion movie

- In iMovie, open a new project and add the picture clip from the Camera Roll to the Timeline
- Save the project with a name
- In GarageBand, share the soundtrack directly to the iMovie using 'Open in...'
- In iMovie, trim the start of the clip so the pictures of the actual metamorphosis are at the same time as the climax in the music
- Trim the end of the clip to shorten it to the length of the soundtrack
- Add the title and credits
- Export the completed stop motion to the Camera Roll.

219

RACE DAY

Man and machine become one.
Capture the action down on the track.

Get your camera down into the action, right onto the stage and into your set to record a car race.

The stages of the project are:

- Creating the soundtrack (GarageBand)
- Building the set
- Recording the pictures (iStopMotion)
- Combining pictures and soundtrack (iMovie).

Watch Race Day stop motion:
www.ipadanimation.net/epub_media4.html

Creating the soundtrack

Car races are typically demonstrations of speed, drama and raw power. The soundtrack needs to convey action – fast and furious!

The GarageBand soundtrack has four tracks of loops and one instrument track. It has a strong beat with distinct surges of energy.

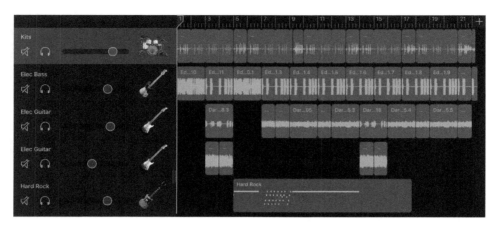

- Start a new song
- Swipe left or right to until you see Audio Recorder. Tap Instrument
- Tap the Sections button and set Section A to 22 bars (about 37 seconds)
- Tap Settings and increase the Tempo to 140 (beats per minute) – *this makes the beats quicker and the sound faster*

- Change the key to D which will slightly raise the pitch of the sounds
- Tap the Tracks button.

Track 1: Audio Recorder with two Drum loops – *Solid 70s Drumset 07* and *Solid 70s Fills 8, 10, 23* and *39*. These loops have similar sounds, but different rhythms. Fill the whole track with a pattern of four bars of the 'solid' loop followed by one bar of a 'fill' loop.

Track 2: Audio Recorder with Bass loops – *Edgy Rock 10* and *11*. These two loops have similar sounds – one is quieter, the other louder. Fill the whole track with a random assortment of these two loops.

Track 3: Audio Recorder with Guitar loops – *Dark and Heavy Riff 04, 05, 06* and *18*. These four loops have similar energetic sounds. Fill the whole track with a random assortment of these loops. Remove some bars leaving gaps to vary the intensity of the overall sound.

Track 4: Audio Recorder with Guitar loops – *Classic Attitude Rock 01* and *18*. This is a second guitar track. Use two short blocks of fast and furious guitar loops to play at the same time as the quieter loops in track 3. The volume for this track is quieter so it doesn't dominate.

These first four tracks give a solid framework of fast aggressive action. The soundtrack needs a small personalisation with some melody.

Track 5: Smart Guitar with *Hard Rock* sound using the *Vintage Drive* and *Robo Flanger* effects. Set to play notes. This track starts in bar 5. **Hold** note D until the sound has ended. In bar 7, **tap** six quick runs of notes G, A, C and D. In bar 9, **hold** note D and **drag vertically** until the sound ends.

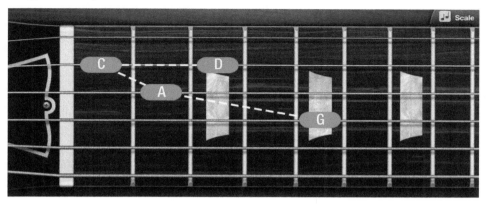

Find the original GarageBand file and the MP3 of this soundtrack in the download.

Building the set

- Build a set using LEGO road plates to form a track
- Add buildings and stands to create interesting viewpoints
- Use a painted cardboard background to ensure the camera can't see beyond the edge of the set
- Adding detail to the set adds overall realism.

Recording the pictures

- Import the soundtrack into iStopMotion (see *Transferring a GarageBand Song* on page 97)
- It is beneficial to be able to check the soundtrack when recording the pictures, but with this type of music-based soundtrack it is not crucial. Listen to the soundtrack and note the timing of significant beat and mood changes. Write the times on paper to reduce touching the iPad
- Choose **camera angles and movements** which match the mood of the soundtrack and change camera positions on the beat of the music to increase the effect of the actions and movements
- Set **speed** to 10 FPS for smooth animation with the minimum number of pictures. As camera movements fit with key points in the soundtrack, the speed can't be changed later

- In many of these angles the camera was placed delicately against props in the set. Use a **remote control** or a **remote camera** to avoid touching the camera
- Devise simple stands using LEGO bricks to support the camera at various positions
- For each recording position, ensure the camera has a good and interesting **picture composition**
- For each recording position, set the **camera focus**. Different camera angles may affect the lighting. Fixed exposure will help maintain a constant brightness.

Camera angles

Change the camera position frequently to convey the fast pace of the car race.

This stop motion has **24 camera angles in 37 seconds**. Constantly changing camera angles convey the feeling of drama at a race track. Aim to change camera angle on the beat of the sound (in our case it was one second). Some camera changes are after 2 beats. There are also a number of image montages.

Here is an outline of some of the camera angles:

Blurry: Build interest at the start. Slowly introduce the race drivers with partial views, including angled camera view and blurry foreground.

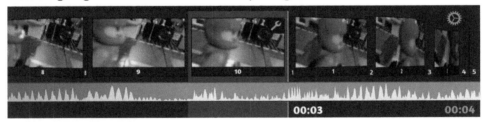

Collage: A short sequence of individual pictures creates a sense of busyness and action.

Drive by: Slide the camera quickly along the track and record pictures using time lapse mode. This provides more connectedness than the above collage sequence.

Build up: Place the camera low on the set. Set manual focus on the race caller and the contestants. Animate each car driving into view. This introduces us to the characters.

Centreline: Sit the camera on the track with the lens above the centreline to show the tension between the characters.

Trackside: Place the camera on a stand at the side of the track as the cars race by. An easy and standard camera view.

Overhead: Place the camera overhead to create a birds eye view. Place a taller table next to the set. Balance a small plank on a raised platform and protruding over the set. Place the camera on the end of the plank to record an overhead view.

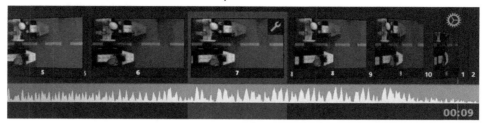

Crowd: The more characters the more realistic the drama. Fill a small grandstand with race fans. Picture by picture, turn their heads to follow the cars.

Closeup: Place the camera down low on the set and show smoke coming off the tires as a car turns a corner.

Handhold: Hold the camera in your hands. Move the cars and then position the camera again. Use the overlay (centre Show option) to align the heads of the drivers with the previous picture.

Dash-cam: Modify the front of a car with additional LEGO bricks to provide support for the camera. The minimum focus distance for the iPad mini is around 6cm. Under the other end of the camera place a wooden stick across the set to assist sliding the camera smoothly. Use time lapse to record the pictures as you firmly hold the camera and drive the car along the track.

Tracking move: Place the camera on a box on the table next to the set. Every picture move the cars along the track, but also slide the box to create a tracking movement. Different effects will be achieved by sliding the box in the same direction as the cars, or in the opposite direction.

Intense: View the cars from behind and between set props. This shows competitiveness between the drivers and the race danger.

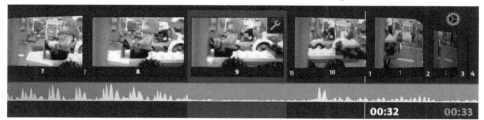

Angle: Place the camera at an angle to create uncertainty.

After recording

- **Export** the clip from iStopMotion to the Camera Roll. Choose the picture quality. In most cases this is HD/Full Size - High Quality 1280 x 720.

If the soundtrack was imported to iStopMotion, the stop motion is complete; otherwise, combine the pictures and soundtrack together in iMovie.

Editing the stop motion movie

- In iMovie, open a new project and add the picture clip from the Camera Roll to the Timeline
- Save the project with a name
- From GarageBand, share the soundtrack directly to the iMovie project using 'Open in...
- In iMovie, add the title and credits
- Export the completed stop motion to the Camera Roll.

Go walkabout with the iPad, or strap it to a vehicle. Record your travel, whether from point A to B or a voyage of discovery.

Time Lapse

Stop motion is a good way to show a journey. It could be in a vehicle, on a skateboard, trolley, bicycle or on foot. The camera is constantly moving. So, the pictures may be sightly blurry but this will improve the fluid motion when played back.

The stages of the project are:

- Recording the pictures (iStopMotion)
- Creating the soundtrack (GarageBand)
- Combining pictures and soundtrack (iMovie).

For this project the iPad was mounted through the sunroof of a car. **Make sure the camera is secured safely** – the author cannot be held responsible for any damage caused by insecure mounting.

Watch Road Trip stop motion:
www.ipadanimation.net/epub_media4.html

Recording the pictures

- Make sure the iPad is **fully charged**, as recording may be limited by the battery charge
- **Mount the camera securely** to the vehicle (or other mode of transport such as a skateboard, trolley or bicycle). Place pieces of wood across the width and height of the car so the iPad can be firmly secured. Use supports such as elastic, duct tape, string and cushions to secure the iPad in place. Every situation will be different. If in doubt, add another tie down, and get someone else to check your mount. Drive slowly at first to test the mount

- Mount the iPad so the **rear camera** is at the top and its view is high enough to record over the bonnet of the car. Avoid recording through the windscreen as the glass will produce reflection and refraction which will reduce the quality of the picture

- Make sure the camera is level with the horizon

- Set the **exposure**. Fixed exposure adjusts the brightness of the picture to compensate for different lighting conditions, such as driving in sunshine or in shadow. Evaluate the results of fixed and continuous exposure before recording

- Check the **white balance**

- Set the **time lapse** interval. A short interval of one second will record enough pictures to have flowing continuity around the many bends in the road.

  If your vehicle has a WiFi connection, or you are recording in a public area or a building with WiFi, you will be able to use an iPod Touch or iPhone as a remote camera. These devices offer many other mounting options because they are smaller, but they have a longer interval between recording pictures

- Drive slowly (40 kph or slower). Travel in straight lines and smooth sweeping curves so the camera is able to follow the route without sudden jolts.

After recording

- Adjust the **playback speed**. In this example, 2707 pictures were recorded during the 45 minute journey. This was many more pictures than expected and meant a revision to the original goal

- We decided to use the first 30 seconds as indicative of the whole journey. At 30 FPS it was not comfortable watching the pictures zoom around tight bends.

There is no right or wrong speed (FPS). Make an artistic choice about which speed gives the best 'feel'. Sometimes the speed is best chosen by playing the pictures with the soundtrack. *We chose 19 FPS*

- **Export** the clip from iStopMotion to the Camera Roll. Choose the picture quality – in most cases this is HD/Full Size - High Quality 1280 x 720.

Creating the soundtrack

Watch the clip and get a feel for the pace and mood of the activity in the pictures. This stop motion is about a journey, going somewhere, on a summer day. The soundtrack should have a carefree pace and be relaxing.

The GarageBand soundtrack has four tracks of loops and one instrument track.

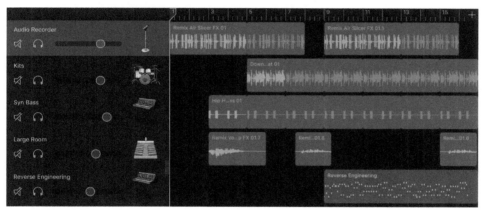

- Start a new song
- Swipe left or right to until you see Audio Recorder. Tap Instrument
- Tap the Sections button and set Section A to 16 bars (about 37 seconds)
- Tap the Tracks button.

Track 1: Audio Recorder with Drum loop – *Remix Air Slicer FX Technibeat*. Remove small sections to allow more variety and interest to the overall soundtrack.

Track 2: Audio Recorder with Drum loop – *Downtempo Bounce Beat*. Start in bar 5 after a complete cycle of the loop in the first track.

Track 3: Audio Recorder with Bass loop – *Hip Hop Mic It Bass*. Start at bar 3.

Track 4: Audio Recorder with Vocal loop – *Remix Vocal Warp FX 01*. This loop builds the sound up or down – a little bit like changing gears on a car. This leads you to expect that something else is coming next, allowing a new type of rhythm element to start.

Place the loop in the track and trim it to three bars, as shown.

231

Place the another copy of the loop and trim it to 2 bars, as shown.

Tap the microphone icon and apply the *Large Room* sound effect to the track.

Track 5: Keyboard with *Reverse Engineering* sound. The soundtrack is personalised with a short melody. The melody should not interfere with the rhythm of the other tracks, but should add 'icing on the cake'.

Slide the Latch to lock as this holds the note until a new note is played.

Turn the Metronome on.

Turn on the Arpeggiator function to add a run of notes higher and lower than the note played.

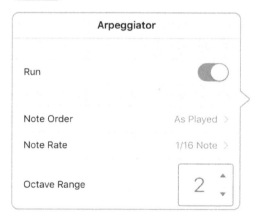

The Arpeggiator creates a unique tune based on the notes you play, but not necessarily including those exact notes. The following music is indicative of a sequence of random notes that can produce a good sound. Experiment and try different note combinations until you are happy with the result.

Raise the Octave to +1. Our example starts on note D4.

Starting in bar 9, play one note on every metronome beat.

Find the original GarageBand file and the MP3 of this soundtrack in the download.

Editing the stop motion movie

- In iMovie, open a new project and add the picture clip from the Camera Roll to the Timeline
- Save the project with a name
- From GarageBand, share the soundtrack directly to the iMovie project using 'Open In'
- In iMovie, trim the picture clip to match the soundtrack, or open the clip in iStopMotion and, if necessary change the speed
- Add the title and credits
- Export the completed stop motion to the Camera Roll.

A 'fly-on-the-wall' style is a great way to record an event such as a concert or ceremony. Start before the first person comes in and end after the last person leaves.

The stages of the project are:

- Recording the pictures (iStopMotion)
- Creating the soundtrack (GarageBand)
- Editing the pictures and combine with soundtrack (iMovie).

Watch Fly on the Wall stop motion:
www.ipadanimation.net/epub_media4.html

Recording the pictures

- Make sure the iPad is **fully charged,** as recording may be limited by the battery charge. If the event is long, check for a power connection
- Find a recording position with a good and interesting **picture composition suitable for the whole event**. Check the position is stable and won't move during the event
- Make sure the camera is secure
- Set the **focus** on the stage area
- Set the **exposure**. With continuous exposure, the pictures will show the changing light conditions as experienced in the event
- Set the **white balance**. We held a sheet of light blue paper in front of the camera to produce a warm yellowish picture
- Calculate and set the **time lapse** recording interval (see *Calculate time lapse interval* on page 169):

    Event – length of the event in seconds (estimated 80 minutes) – 4800 seconds
    Length – the pictures need to match the length of the soundtrack (56 seconds)

> *Rate* – a playback speed of 30FPS
> *Time Lapse interval* = 4800 / (56 x 30) = 2.8 seconds.

- Tap the Record button to start recording, then don't touch the iPad again during the event
- After the event, tap the Stop button to end the recording.

After recording

- Set the playback speed (frame rate) to 30 FPS. We had recorded 1632 pictures
- Export the clip to the Camera Roll. Choose the picture quality. In most cases this is HD/Full Size - High Quality 1280 x 720.

Creating the soundtrack

The soundtrack created in GarageBand has three tracks of loops and three instrument tracks:

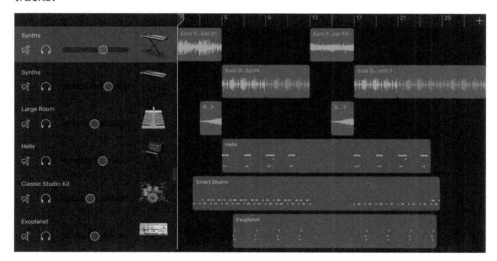

- Start a new song
- Swipe left or right to until you see Audio Recorder. Tap Instrument
- Tap the Sections button and set Section A to 28 bars (about 56 seconds)
- Tap the Tracks button.

Track 1: Audio Recorder with Synth loop – *Euro Vox Slicer 01*. Start the soundtrack with one cycle (four bars). Add a second cycle of four bars starting in bar 12.

Track 2: Audio Recorder with Synth loop – *Euro Odd Mechanical Synth*. Starting in bar 5 fill all parts of the track except where there is a loop in track 1.

This gives a complete base from two different synths.

235

Track 3: Audio Recorder with Vocal loop – *Remix Reverse Vocal FX*. Add two short loops (two bars each) aligned with the end of the loops in track 1 to help build up the sound and accentuate a new phase in the song.

Place the loop in the track and trim it in half as shown.

Track 4: Smart Keyboard using *Helix* keyboard with *Autoplay setting 3*. Only eight notes are actually played in the track. All the rest is from the Autoplay option. In each of the bars 5, 7, 9, 11, 17, 19, 21 and 23 tap note C and immediately tap the note again to stop the Autoplay, so only a few notes are heard.

Track 5: Smart Drum with *Classic Studio Kit* sound. Simple effect with only two drums in kit (snare and base drum). Starts in bar 3.

Track 6: Smart Bass with *Exoplanet* sound and with *Autoplay setting 4*. In each of the bars 6, 8, 10, 12, 18, 20, 22 and 24, tap note C and immediately tap the note again to stop the Autoplay so only a few notes are heard.

Tap Settings and turn on Fade Out which will gradually decrease the volume at the end of the last track.

Find the original GarageBand file and the MP3 of this soundtrack in the download.

Editing the stop motion movie

- In iMovie, open a new project and add the picture clip from the Camera Roll to the Timeline
- Save the project with a name
- From GarageBand, share the soundtrack directly to the iMovie project using 'Open in...'
- In iMovie, trim the picture clip to match the soundtrack, or open the clip in iStopMotion and change the speed if necessary
- Add the title and credits
- Export the completed stop motion to the Camera Roll.

Turn something mundane into a fun and quirky occasion. Look for ways to add humour and surprises.

The stages of the project are:

- Creating the soundtrack (GarageBand)
- Recording the pictures (iStopMotion)
- Editing pictures and combining with soundtrack (iMovie).

 **Watch Sports Day stop motion:**
www.ipadanimation.net/epub_media4.html

Creating the soundtrack

The GarageBand soundtrack has four tracks of loops.

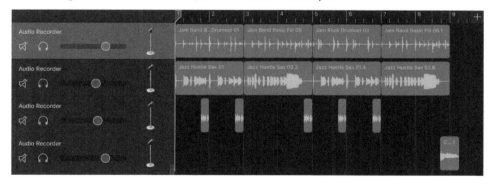

- Start a new song
- Swipe left or right to until you see Audio Recorder. Tap Instrument
- Tap the Sections button and set Section A to 9 bars (about 18 seconds)
- Tap the Tracks button.

Track 1: Audio Recorder with Drum loop – *Jam Band Basic Drumset 01* and *03*, and *Jam Band Basic Fill 06*. Fill eight bars with alternating loops.

Track 2: Audio Recorder with Woodwind loop – *Jazz Hustle Sax 01* and *02*. Fill eight bars with alternating loops.

Track 3: Audio Recorder with Guitars loop – *Jazz Hustle Guitar 01*. Trim the loop to one short strum – around quarter of a bar long.

Place five occurrences of this along the track.

Tap Track Controls and set the Echo Level slider for this track to around 40%.

Track 4: Audio Recorder with Vocal loop – *Cuban Sons Horns 01*. Trim the loop to the first horn blast – around half a bar long.

Place this at the end of the track, after the last significant sound in track 2.

Find the original GarageBand file and the MP3 of this soundtrack in the download.

Recording the pictures

- Create a clear set and remove unnecessary clutter
- Plan the sequence of animation actions as if they are the story
- Discuss with the person where they should look, what they should do with their hands etc.
- Use a **remote control** or a **remote camera** to avoid touching the camera. Alternatively use time **lapse mode** with an interval of around 5 seconds – long enough for the helper to enter the set, move the prop and exit the set
- For each recording position, ensure the camera has a good and interesting **picture composition**
- Move the camera periodically for a closer view of a specific action
- For each recording position, set the **camera focus** and **exposure**. Different camera angles may affect the lighting. Fixed exposure will help maintain a constant brightness

- This type of stop motion requires a helper to move on and off the set between pictures. **One of the biggest challenges for the helper is to move every part of their body completely out the camera view, every picture. The**  **helper needs to plan a position to withdraw to where they will not block light from any direct or indirect source**

- Remember you are not recording sound so you can talk at the pictures are recorded and give instructions to your helpers.

After recording

- **Review** the clip. Delete individual problem pictures, such as a stray limb (of the helper) or a significant shadow or lighting change

- Adjust the **playback speed** (Clip Settings) to suit the soundtrack. In this example, we recorded 342 pictures which required a play speed of 21 FPS to match the length of the soundtrack

- **Export** the clip from iStopMotion to the Camera Roll. Choose the picture quality – in most cases this is HD/Full Size - High Quality 1280 x 720.

Editing the stop motion movie

- In iMovie, open a new project and add the picture clip from the Camera Roll to the Timeline

- Save the project with a name

- In GarageBand, share the soundtrack directly to the iMovie project using 'Open in...'

- Add the title and credits

- Export the completed stop motion to the Camera Roll.

Other ideas for this type of stop motion

Add interest to event recordings, such as prize giving, sports day, field trip or wedding, with an interlude of a stop motion sequence:

- A certificate doing a dance as it 'climbs' into an envelope before presentation
- A flower arrangement coming together one flower at a time
- A ribbon unrolling and forming letters or shapes
- Sports balls coming out of a storage shed all by themselves
- Wedding video – two pairs of shoes walking towards each other
- A cake being cut up and pieces removed
- An animated sports team photo with socks dancing up and down
- A golf ball rolling a very weird path on its way to a hole-in-one
- A table setting itself before a meal
- A lawn mowing itself
- A fence painting itself.

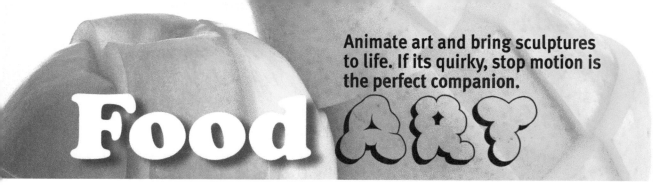

Animate art and bring sculptures to life. If its quirky, stop motion is the perfect companion.

Food ART

Stop motion is a good way to create a visual artwork of the progressive completion of a piece of physical artwork. The clip may be a work of art in itself, an effect for a music video, or an interlude in a movie.

The stages of the project are:

- Recording the pictures (iStopMotion)
- Creating the soundtrack (GarageBand)
- Combining the pictures and soundtrack (iMovie).

Watch Food Art stop motion:
www.ipadanimation.net/epub_media4.html

Recording the pictures

This type of project can be recorded in one iStopMotion clip, or if the artwork is larger, the recording can be done in several clips and edited together in iMovie.

Creating a reference

- On a large table place the camera at an angle so it does not see beyond the edge of the table
- Make sure the camera is held securely in a stand. Make sure you can touch the screen to record a picture without moving the iPad, or use a **remote control** or a **remote camera**

- Set the **focus**
- Set the **exposure**. Fixed exposure will help maintain a constant brightness
- Using the perspective of the camera as a reference, create the final design or an approximation of it. Grid lines may be useful to achieve a balanced **picture composition**

- Record this as a temporary first picture
- Clear the design back to the starting point and record a picture. This will become the first picture once the temporary first picture is deleted
- Set the Show option (Clip Settings) to **overlay** (middle button) so it shows a combination of a recorded picture and the camera view

- Swipe the Timeline back to the first picture
- Place the next object. Notice the ghosted image of the hand placing the object into alignment with the first recorded picture

- Record the picture
- Repeat the last three steps to build up the complete artwork
- When all pictures have been recorded, delete the reference picture.

This type of stop motion may suit a very slow speed of one frame per second. This is the slowest speed iStopMotion offers. If you want a slower speed, eg one frame every two seconds, duplicate each frame. This can be done later. **Duplicating frames ensures they are identical, whereas recording two frames allows the possibility of slight difference in lighting between the two pictures.**

Recording pictures without reference

It is often not practical to build the artwork first. So make the best assessment of the final dimensions of the artwork and position the camera so the artwork won't run off the edge of the screen.

Recording pictures in reverse

Depending on the nature of the artwork, eg a stacked arrangement of items, it may be easier to build the entire artwork first. Position the camera to show the height and width of the work and record the pictures as the artwork is dismantled.

Tap the Actions button in the Timeline and select 'Reverse Order of Frames' to reverse the order of all the pictures.

After recording

- Adjust the **playback speed** (frame rate) so the pictures look their best – *we used 1 FPS*
- **Export** the clip from iStopMotion to the Camera Roll. Choose the picture quality – in most cases this is HD/Full Size - High Quality 1280 x 720.

Creating the soundtrack

There is a certain weirdness about the whole concept of this artwork so we are looking for a weirdness in the sound. The soundtrack should not draw attention to itself, but highlight the art.

The GarageBand soundtrack has two tracks with loops.

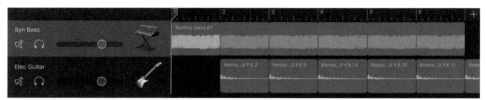

- Start a new song
- Swipe left or right to until you see Audio Recorder. Tap Instrument
- Tap the Sections button and set Section A to 9 bars (about 9 seconds for this scene)
- Tap Settings and increase the Tempo to 240 (beats per minute).

  Changing the tempo changes the number of beats per minute which changes the length of a bar. With this faster tempo, each bar is now one second long
- Tap the Tracks button.

Track 1: Synth bass loop – *Techno Bass.*

Track 2: Guitar loop – *Remix Guitar Hit FX.*

One of the advantages of loops is they adapt to changes in the tempo. The tempo for this song is very fast yet the loop maintains the original pitch.

Both loops are one bar long (one second) and repeat in time with each new picture (1 FPS).

Find the original GarageBand file and the MP3 of this soundtrack in the download.

Editing the stop motion movie

- In iMovie, open a new project and add the picture clip from the Camera Roll to the Timeline
- Save the project with a name
- In GarageBand, share the soundtrack directly to the iMovie using 'Open in…'
- In iMovie, add the title and credits
- Export the completed stop motion to the Camera Roll.

Write your own story: develop characters, add a crisis... what will happen?

My Story

The best way to feature characters in stop motion is to engage them in a story. Write the story first and record it as a soundtrack so you have a reference for recording the pictures.

The stages of the project are:

- Developing the story
- Recording the dialogue (GarageBand)
- Creating a soundtrack (GarageBand)
- Building the set
- Making the characters
- Recording the pictures to match the soundtrack (iStopMotion).

Watch My Story (Go Girl) stop motion:
www.ipadanimation.net/epub_media4.html

Developing a story

Improvising the script

In its simplest form, a story can be told with one sentence for each of these seven questions:

1 **Where are you?** *or* **What do you feel? What do you see? What are you doing?**
2 **What happens?**
3 **What do you do about it?**
4 **What stops you?**
5 **What is the worst outcome?**
6 **What is your last chance for success?**
7 **What is the final outcome?**

The entire three-part story can be told in as little as seven sentences. This also ensures that every sentence is vital to the story development. Download a printable copy of the story outline from *www.ipadanimation.net/store.html*.

Here is an example of a script which follows the above questions:

> 1) Ah, this is the life – a picnic.
>
> 2) (butterfly eats lunch, shown with pictures)
>
> 3) Come back with my lunch.
>
> 4) Slow down. You're too fast for me.
>
>   You can't catch me (butterfly)
>
> 5) This is the worst day of my life…
>
> 6) …unless, I use… (throws book)
>
> 7) Yeah, go girl. Who's awesome now. Aha a, aha a.
>
>   I don't want to be a bookmark (butterfly)

Even if care is taken to record in a quiet room, there may be a small amount of background noise. If you want the best recording, use a USB microphone.

Writing the script

A more common approach to creating a script involves writing it down. When the end of the story is known, the first part can be revised. The full script can be checked, and edited, before recording the dialogue:

- Using a story outline, write the events in the story
- Determine which characters you need and the artwork/props required
- Write the lines of dialogue (some of the seven questions might require more than one sentence). Remember that the more dialogue, the more time required to animate
- Make the start of a story interesting or exciting to catch the audience's attention
- Read through the script. Ensure the story development is clear and has the right pace
- Remove unnecessary words.

Recording the dialogue

Find the quietest space you can (see *Sound versus noise* on page 40).

Make sure you know how to use a microphone (see *Recording with a microphone* on page 44).

For more information on recording dialogue, see *Recording voice* on page 37.

- Start a new GarageBand song
- Tap the Audio Recorder, Tap Voice
- Tap the Sections button and set Section A to Automatic
- Record each sentence of dialogue as a separate clip as they often require a different expression and voice tone
- **It is important that the stop motion dialogue is clear because much of the clarity of the story comes from the audio**
- **Listen carefully to ensure each word is clear and the pronunciation is accurate. Have a breath between sentences. Record another take if required – allow two seconds of silence between takes**
- Trim each clip for the best take
- Drag the first dialogue clip along the track to make allowance for title music. Position it to start at bar 3 (this can be adjusted more precisely after the music is added)
- Drag the other clips along their respective tracks to adjust the timing. Some sentences should flow like a conversation, others allow time for actions to increase tension before the hero makes a move. Add gaps for characters (and the audience) to ponder a situation.

Recording group improvisation

This type of story development can be completed by individuals or as a group. **Because everyone will contribute one sentence to the story (idea and voice), the story belongs to the whole group.** Reinforce that this is 'our story' and it is important that everyone helps everyone else deliver their line, whether through suggestions of ideas, encouragement or being quiet during recording. Here is one way to improvise the story as a group (ideally seven people, but can work with up to 14 people):

- Canvas the group for suggestions about where the story could take place. Choose a location which seems workable and agreeable to most of the group, or is suited to your purpose

- Have one person stand in front of the microphone. To avoid distraction, have them face you with their back to the group. Ask them, in character, to say their answer a statement about where they are, eg *"Wow, this place is so huge"*, *"It's nice to get two minutes peace and quiet"*

  Without the need to read from a written script, people will be able to put all their effort into expression and voice tone. Record one sentence at a time as they may require a different emotion, eg happy, scared, frustrated, despairing or victorious

- If required, record another 'take' to ensure each person gives their dramatic best

- Keep descriptions general so the soundtrack can be animated with different interpretations by sub-groups. Some will plan their story on the moon, others in a forest or in a large box

- Ask each person to contribute the next part of the story. When they stand in front of you, quickly summarise the story so far, to help them get into the situation. Then prompt them for their response to the next question.

  Each person can answer their question from the point of view that makes sense to them. Most people will say their lines as if they are the lead character, which because every line is spoken with a different mood works well. Also, different voices become less noticeable when the same character is seen speaking them.

Creating the soundtrack

Once the dialogue is recorded and edited, it is time to add the sound effects and music. The overall requirements for music to accompany the dialogue are:

- Music for the title at the start
- Background music for the duration of the dialogue
- Sound effects, if required
- Music at the end for the credits.

In addition to the two tracks of dialogue, the GarageBand soundtrack has two tracks of loops and four instrument tracks:

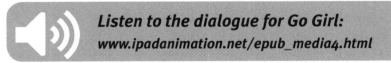

Listen to the dialogue for Go Girl:
www.ipadanimation.net/epub_media4.html

Recording the dialogue

- In GarageBand Start a new song
- Swipe left or right to until you see Audio Recorder

- Tap Voice
- Turn the **Metronome off, the Count-in off and set Sections to automatic** before recording with the microphone.

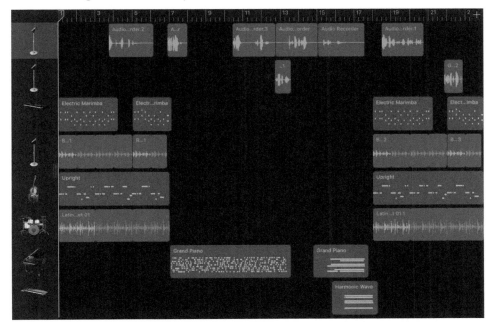

Track 1: Audio Recorder for dialogue (girl).

Track 2: Audio Recorder for dialogue (butterfly).

Track 3: Keyboard with *Electric Marimba* sound.

Track 4: Audio Recorder with Guitar loop – *Brazilian Cavaquinho 01*.

Track 5: Smart Bass with *Upright* sound and *Autoplay setting 2*.

Track 6: Audio Recorder with (drum) Kit loop – *Latin Danza Drumset 01*.

Track 7: Keyboard with *Grand Piano* sound. This is played on a real keyboard.

Track 8: Keyboard with *Harmonic Wave* sound.

 Find the original GarageBand file and the MP3 of this soundtrack in the download.

Building the set

The set for this stop motion comprises one large painted background.

Flat or curved set

The background can be used:

- **Flat** – more suitable for 2D work, and requiring an overhead camera

- **Curved in a frame** – more suitable for 3D work. The curve hides any horizon line that might otherwise be marked by a join in the background sheets.

Making the characters

The two most popular mediums for character development are LEGO and Plasticine. Other useful mediums are whiteboard illustration, coloured paper cut outs and other character toys. In this example we use Plasticine.

2D or 3D characters

Plasticine characters can be moulded with three dimensional shapes. They can be animated to walk and move, but require a bottom-heavy mass to stand up and hold their balance, ie fat legs and big feet.

For 3D modelling, use a wire armature to form the basic shape.

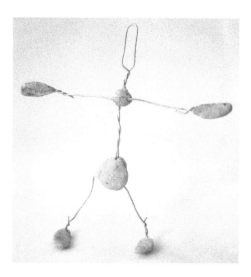

In this case, we used 2D models which lay flat on the background. **With 2D models, gravity is your friend** – characters can run and jump and won't fall over. Butterflies can fly without strings or supports.

- Use a roller to flatten pieces of Plasticine in each colour

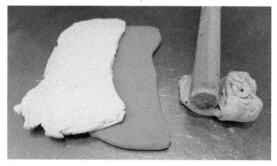

- Use a blunt blade to cut out the basic shape of the character. You may have a cookie cutter which is the right shape
- Press wire clips into the underside to securely hold pieces of plasticine together

- Use wooden tools to sculpt the shape of the character

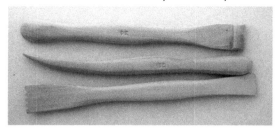

- When animating Plasticine, the mouth can be moulded to form different mouth shapes to convey talking

- Another option for animating talking is to make a different head for each expression. Hide the join between the heads and body is under the neckline of the dress

- Use beads for eyes as they hold their shape and provide a real focus for the character. When animating, use a skewer to move the eyes.

Adding the soundtrack

At the start of this book you created a soundtrack and saved it into iStopMotion. To access it, tap the Audio button and then tap Audio Library.

The soundtrack will appear at the top of the list (with the name you gave it in GarageBand). Tap the soundtrack name. The soundtrack appears along the bottom of the Timeline as a blue line (waveform).

Before recording the pictures, note when each scene starts. This will enable you to work efficiently with the iPad; recording a whole scene at a time while minimising the risk of bumping the iPad:

- Tap the Play button to listen to the soundtrack. Be ready to tap the button again to stop as soon as you hear the first word of each sentence

- Swipe left or right through the Timeline and, using the blue line as a reference, locate the exact start of the sentence. Note the seconds (large number along the bottom) and the frame (small numbers under each picture). The example below shows 4 seconds 2 frames – write this as '4.2'

Start of each scene	
title	0.0 seconds
1	4.2
2	9.6
3	15.4
(chase)	22.4
4	28.2
5	33.0
6	40.3
7	51.6

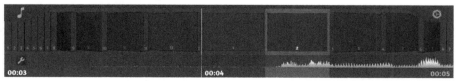

253

- Repeat these steps for each sentence.

Also note the timing (second and frame) when you want action sequences to start, and any other place where pictures and sound need to match.

If you want a very accurate match between pictures and soundtrack within each scene, continually refer to the blue sound waveform as you record the pictures.

Recording the pictures

This type of stop motion has a story about characters and their relationships. Every decision about picture composition and camera position is to make the story clear.

- Listen to the soundtrack and write down the time when each scene starts
- Tape the background on a low table
- Place the camera on a board suspended above the table

- Set the **speed** to at least 10 FPS for smooth animation. As the pictures will be recorded to match the soundtrack, the speed can't be changed later
- Use a **remote control, remote camera** or **time lapse** to avoid touching the camera.

The opening scene

The first pictures you record need to get people interested in the story. Choose a picture composition which is simple and suitable for the title. We'll add the title onto the pictures later in iMovie although sometimes you may want to animate it and this needs to be done first.

The opening scene may be a simple movement such as a car driving by, or a view of the background. Don't start animating the story, and in most cases don't show the characters, until the start of the first sentence.

At the start of each scene

Tap the Settings button and tap the right 'Show' button.

Listen to the next part of the soundtrack, eg *character talks for 3 seconds then walks to the door.*

Decide how that part of the story should 'look' and arrange the characters and props.

Decide where the character will move during the scene and position the camera to clearly show the movement.

Check the picture composition and make sure it is easy to see which character is talking.

Set the camera focus.

- For each recording position, ensure the camera has a good and interesting **picture composition**. From time to time change the height of the board for a different camera view to help tell the story

- Set the Show option (Clip Settings) to **overlay** (middle button) to show a combination of the recorded picture and the camera view. This will show the animation movements – what moves and what doesn't

- For each recording position, set the **camera focus on the character's eyes**
- For each recording position set the **exposure**. Different camera angles may affect the lighting. Fixed exposure will help maintain a constant brightness.

After the last scene

After the last sentence has been spoken there are two things to achieve:

- Record extra pictures to fill all the spaces under the soundtrack to show a closing story action such as the character walking or driving into the sunset.

  These extra pictures will allow the music to finish, and if the credits are to be added in iMovie, provide closing pictures over which to add the names. If you are short on time, record one picture and duplicate it to fill all the spaces

- Add the names of the people who made the stop motion in the credits. The credits can be animated now or simply added as text in iMovie.

After recording

- **Review** all clips. Delete individual problem pictures, such as a hand in shot or a significant shadow or light change.

  For each deleted picture duplicate one in the same scene to maintain the match between the pictures and the soundtrack

- **Export** the clip to the Camera Roll. Choose the picture quality. In most cases this is HD/Full Size - High Quality 1280 x 720.

Editing the stop motion movie

Even if the stop motion is complete with pictures and sound, use iMovie to add the title and credits:

- In iMovie, open a new project and add the picture clip from the Camera Roll to the Timeline
- Add the title and credits
- Export the completed stop motion to the Camera Roll.

WATERCYCLE

Up, down, up, down.
The wonders of the water cycle.

Non-fiction topics

Stop motion is an excellent medium to communicate information – facts and details. Whether it is a documentary, research, investigation or explanation of a process, follow the same recording process as for a dramatic story.

The stages of the project are:

- Writing the script
- Recording the dialogue (GarageBand)
- Creating the soundtrack (GarageBand)
- Building the set
- Recording the pictures (iStopMotion)
- Editing the movie (iMovie).

Watch Water Cycle stop motion:
www.ipadanimation.net/epub_media4.html

Writing the script

- Research the facts on the topic and determine which ones you want to present
- Arrange each point in logical order
- Simplify each point. Over the page is the script for the water cycle used in this example:

257

> The water cycle is the continuous movement of water – on, above and below the surface of the earth.
>
> You might say it starts as rain. Sometimes it is snow or hail.
>
> The droplets of water run downhill and join together making streams and rivers - which run into the ocean.
>
> The radiation of the sun converts the water into water vapour – which rises into the atmosphere.
>
> Cooler temperatures in the sky cause water vapour to condense into clouds.
>
> And then it starts all over again.
>
> Here's a cool fact: the approximate annual global rainfall is 505,000km^3.
>
> That is enough to fill…well…lots of bathtubs.

- Read the script and listen for any words which are difficult to pronounce. Note how long it takes to read, allowing gaps for actions and music (on average expect two words per second – a hundred word script will produce a movie around one minute long). The longer the script, the more time required to animate.

Recording the dialogue

- In GarageBand Start a new song
- Swipe left or right to until you see Audio Recorder
- Tap Voice
- Turn the **Metronome off, the Count-in off and set Sections to automatic** before recording with the microphone.

This type of stop motion requires a clear narration voice with an even pace and tone:

- Record each sentence as a separate clip to allow for the best tone and expression
- Listen carefully to ensure each word is clear and the pronunciation is accurate. Record another take if required
- Trim each clip for the best take
- Drag the first dialogue clip to make allowance for title music. Position it to start at bar 3 (this can be adjusted more accurately after the music is added)
- Drag the other clips along their respective tracks to adjust the timing. Some sentences should flow like a conversation, others allow time for actions
- If you need more tracks, drag clips vertically into another Audio Recorder track.

Creating the soundtrack

The overall requirements for audio to accompany the dialogue are:

- Sound effects
- Music for the title at the start
- Background music for the duration of the dialogue
- Music at the end for the credits.

In addition to the dialogue, the GarageBand soundtrack has three instrument tracks:

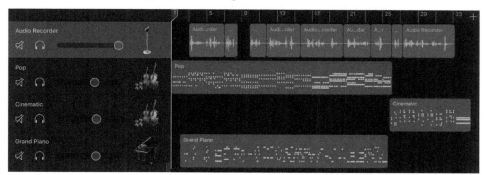

The music for this soundtrack has been composed to create impressions of flowing movement – like water.

Track 2: Smart Strings with Pop sound.

Track 3: Smart Strings with *Cinematic* sound. This is the same instrument as track 2, but with a different type of sound to indicate a new phase in the information.

Track 4: Keyboard with *Grand Piano* sound. This is played on a real keyboard.

Find the original GarageBand file and the MP3 of this soundtrack in the download.

Building the set

Many of the origami models used instructions from *www.origami-instructions.com*.

Squares of unfolded origami paper were used to add texture and interest to the minimalist stage set.

This is a fairly large set and better suited for the floor than on a table. Use large sheets of coloured card to surround the set.

Title sequence

The title sequence ends with a scene change using clouds. The clouds were placed on a sheet of blue card, supported on two blocks of wood, so that it could slide over the sheet of green card.

Cotton wool makes excellent clouds.

Aerial view

An overhead rig was used to suspend the iPad on strings hung over a pole. Pictures were recorded using **time lapse** as the strings were slowly and smoothly released to record the raindrop's view of falling to earth.

Recording the pictures

- Secure the camera in a stable **stand**

- Set the **speed** to 12 FPS for smooth animation. As camera movements fit with key points in the soundtrack, the speed can't be changed later

- Use a **remote control**, remote camera or **time lapse** to avoid touching the camera

- For each recording position, ensure the camera has a good and interesting **picture composition**

- For each recording position, set the **camera focus** and **exposure**. Different camera angles may affect the lighting. Fixed exposure will help maintain a constant brightness

- At the start and end of each clip, record an additional one second of pictures as this gives more options for editing and using transitions in iMovie

- Set the Show option (Clip Settings) to **overlay** (middle button) so it shows a combination of a recorded picture and the camera view

- When building up a complete image in stages, start with the whole layout to ensure it is balanced and centered. Record a picture as a reference then clear the set

- As you place each new element, swipe the Timeline back to the reference picture.

261

The water cycle stop motion is one minute and 16 seconds. It has 912 pictures and is recorded to play at a speed of 12 FPS.

The pictures for this stop motion were recorded in several clips. In each clip, the position of the soundtrack was adjusted with a negative offset (see *Audio options* on page 159) to match the start of the scene.

After recording

- **Review** all clips. Delete individual problem pictures, such as a hand in shot or a significant shadow or lighting change

- For each deleted picture duplicate one in the same scene to maintain the match between the pictures and the soundtrack

- **Export** each clip from iStopMotion to the Camera Roll. Choose the picture quality – in most cases this is HD/Full Size - High Quality 1280 x 720.

Editing the stop motion movie

In iMovie, open a new project:

- Add the soundtrack to the Timeline

- Add each picture clip from the Camera Roll to the Timeline

- Tap the waveform button to view a visual representation of the soundtracks.

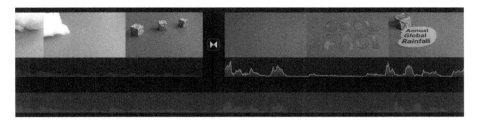

The duplicate soundtracks are useful to ensure the clips are placed in the right position. If the background and clip waveforms are not in alignment, we'll fix this over the next steps

- Add transitions as appropriate – we used several cross dissolve transitions. Transitions affect how closely the clips fit to each other and may change the alignment of the clip soundtrack to the background soundtrack causing an echo – we'll fix this later

  Split the picture clip designated for the credits into segments for the names. In each clip set a title style – we used the Opening style (Simple theme). Type the text

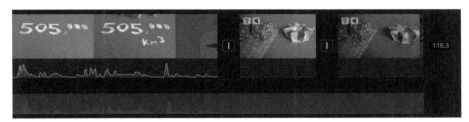

- Starting at the first clip, adjust the trim points (see *Precise editing* on page 191) to move the alignment of the soundtrack waveform to match the waveform of the background soundtrack

- When the background and chip waveforms are in alignment, from the start of the movie, tap each clip then tap the speaker icon at the bottom of the screen to mute the clip soundtrack so only the background soundtrack (green bar) is heard

- Add the title and credits
- Export the completed stop motion to the Camera Roll.

Contribute to the Water Cycle Project:
www.ipadanimation.net/watercycleproject.html

263

264

TITLES and CREDITS

The title and credits are important parts of a stop motion movie and are often added last. It can be easier to decide the title when you've seen the completed stop motion. You can never be sure of the complete list of people needing to be acknowledged in the credits until after the work has been done.

There are two common methods for adding the title and credits:

- Animate them in iStopMotion
- Add them to the stop motion pictures, in iMovie.

Watch titles and credits for stop motion movies:
www.ipadanimation.net/epub_media4.html

Here are some general comments about titles:

- Think about what is seen behind the actual text. Choose a bland image such as the sky or a wall that won't conflict with the text. Using a blurry image can help

- Avoid pictures with people in the foreground as the text may go over their faces

- Keep titles short, eg *'Riders'* is better than *'The people who rode from the desert'*

- Choose a title that is relevant, accurate and creates intrigue. Don't give away the outcome of the story, eg *'Trouble ahead'* may be better than *'Slaying the dragon all by myself'*

- The full title should remain visible long enough so people have time to read it. For example, at least two seconds of introductory pictures to set the scene, three seconds displaying the title and two seconds to transition to the first scene.

- If the stop motion is longer, the title sequence can be longer.

Titles in iStopMotion

An animated title is a nice start to a stop motion movie (see *Water Cycle project* on page 257). But if you want the whole stop motion in the iStopMotion file, the title needs to be decided at the start because it should be animated first.

Alternatively, create the title as a separate clip and edit them together in iMovie. One advantage of creating the title as a separate clip is that you can use a different speed.

Have fun animating titles and credits but don't make them a bigger production than the actual stop motion. It may take longer to animate them than to create them in iMovie, but if you keep the effect simple it need not take a lot of time.

Titles in iMovie

iMovie offers a range of professional styles and effects. The range is small, but the titles are quick and easy to use and look good.

For the **title**, it is best to record bland or blank pictures at the start of the stop motion ready for the title to be overlaid. The soundtrack should allow up to ten seconds for the title before the first sentence. Recording pictures for the title helps keep the rest of the pictures in sync with the timing of the soundtrack.

For the **credits**, if the soundtrack continues after the last scene, record extra pictures in iStopMotion until the music has finished.

Animating titles in iStopMotion

Titles are important because they identify and personalise your stop motion. Their main purpose is functional – to show the name of your stop motion. If you've got time why not make them fun as well?

- Plan the size and position of your title so it is large on screen and logically aligned. If you are animating individual letters, do a test to make sure you won't run out of room. Sometimes you can start with the full title and record it backwards

- **Make sure letters are clearly formed so they are legible and double check your spelling**

- Use reference markers, out of camera view, to assist movement and alignment

- Use a suitable rig to ensure any camera or text movements are smooth and even

There are many ways to animate a title in stop motion. Watch the examples in this clip and then read the following notes about them.

Rice

Titles can be formed out of almost anything – rice, pasta, lollies, sand etc. Place the camera on a board suspended above the table. Tape paper to the table showing the area visible to the camera. Draw guides on the paper to help align the letters.

This title was recorded using **time lapse with a one second interval**. In this case, we wanted to see hands forming the letter shapes. This style of title could also be recorded without visible hands by using a longer time lapse interval.

Cut out words/letters

Print the title at a large size on coloured paper. Cut out the words and animate them moving into position to form the title.

For shorter titles, cut out the letters and animate them moving into position to spell the word.

Start with the complete title arranged on a table with good spacing and margins within the screen.

Use a **remote control** to record pictures without touching the iPad.

Record enough pictures so the full title is visible for at least two seconds.

Animate the movement of the letters off the screen or into a starting position.

When recording is complete, tap the Action button on the current thumbnail and select 'reverse order' so the title builds up.

This approach can be used with letters painted on toy blocks, cut into fruit or out of bread slices etc.

LEGO

LEGO bricks can be used for shorter titles. Build up the words using LEGO, or start with the words already built and break them down.

Record enough pictures so the full title is visible for at least two seconds. For the build-up or break-down stage add or remove several bricks between pictures so it doesn't take too long.

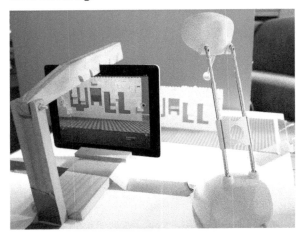

Record the whole sequence using **time lapse** with a three second interval, or longer. This interval should be sufficient to knock several bricks off the wall and move hands out of the way of camera and lights. Or use a **remote control** to avoid touching the camera.

If a picture is recorded with hands in shot wait until a second picture is recorded without hands. Afterwards, delete any pictures showing hands.

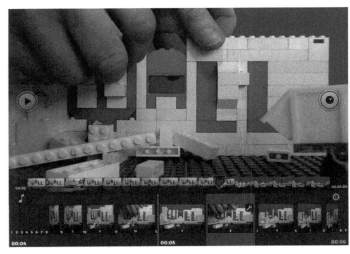

In some cases, it is easiest to record pictures breaking down the words, then reverse the order so they play 'backwards'. If you are going to reverse the order, make sure movements by characters are also backwards.

Printouts

A title was designed on a computer and printed on four pages with various parts removed. The effect is to have the title flicker on like a neon sign. We used 30 FPS to achieve a fast flicker effect.

Use a **remote control** to record pictures without touching the iPad. Record one picture of each sheet in this sequence – sheet **1**, 2, *1*, **2**, 3, *2*, 3, *2*, **3**, 4, *3*, **4**.

Use the overlay to ensure the pages align perfectly so the elements are in the same place in each picture.

Duplicate pictures to create the flickering build up effect. Duplicate at least one second of each sheet indicated in **bold**. Leave all sheets indicated in italics as single pictures to create the flicker effect. Duplicate all other sheets between three and six times. Duplicating pictures is better than recording identical pictures as it eliminates the possibility of changes in lighting conditions.

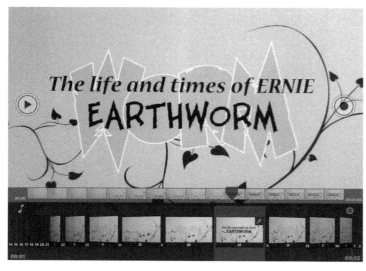

 A variation of this method uses several versions of the title word in slightly different styles or fonts. They could event be hand drawn. The titles will purposely flicker as the different sheets are displayed.

Poster

Add the title elements into a poster or artwork, eg as a sign on a building. Place the iPad on a board suspended above the table. Slide the poster over the table to let the camera pan across the scene and then stop to focus on the text.

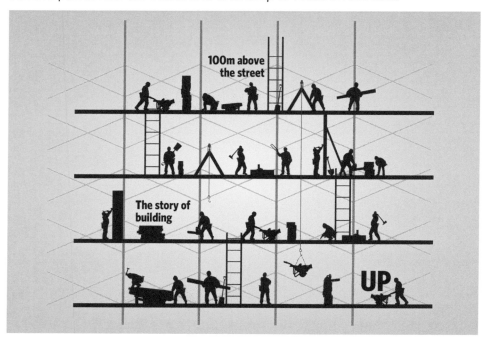

Use **time lapse** or **remote control** to avoid touching the camera.

This approach could also be recorded in iMovie as video, but iStopMotion allows much greater control over picture exposure, white balance and focus.

Whiteboard

Push and pull the hand-drawn letters into place. Let your hands be visible to the camera as if the whiteboard markings are tangible objects.

Artwork

Paint the title on a canvas, assemble it as a collage, sculpt it into sand, stick Post-it® notes on a wall etc.

Credits in iStopMotion

At the end of your stop motion you may, or may not, have people to acknowledge.

If you made the stop motion by yourself, you might say:

> Written and Animated by
> YOUR NAME

or

> Animation by
> YOUR NAME

If there are many people to thank, sort them into an order like this:

> Story/script by NAME
>
> List of characters and voices
> CHARACTER/S – NAME/S
>
> Props made by NAME/S
>
> Animation by NAME/S
>
> Sound recorded/music by NAME
>
> Music credits (copyright etc)
>
> Anyone else you need to thank
>
> Produced by NAME
>
> Directed by NAME
>
> Year

If people have more than one role just state their most important role.

What is a director?

The director is the person who has the main ideas about making the movie. They have the vision of how the story should be told; what the set should look like, the music and sound effects and the camera angles.

What is a producer?

A producer is responsible for the equipment, the people and the budget.

Set up

- Think about the background for the credits. Use something plain like a wall, or create a backdrop which won't make it hard to read the words. It could be a still image or a subtle animation that won't detract from the words

- Use a suitable rig for the camera or the sheet of words to control the movement. Above all, the credits need to be readable

- However you animate them, **each person's name needs to be on screen for a minimum of two seconds – three seconds if the words are moving.**

Cut out names

Print the names on a sheet of coloured card and cut them out in small groups in shapes. Place the cards into the scene. and record one picture of each. Duplicate the picture so it displays for three seconds.

Animate them on a table sliding past the camera, or attach them to objects on your desk. Using **time lapse** with a short interval, zoom to each name for two seconds.

Scrolling credits

Scrolling text is the most common method used for movie credits. iMovie does not offer this feature, but we can animate it with stop motion.

Print the list of credits down the centre of a large sheet of paper – A3 or larger. Leave a large margin at the top and bottom of the sheet so the start and finish doesn't show the edge of the page.

Place the iPad on a board suspended above the table at a height where the text is in focus and the longest line fits in the screen. Tape a strip of wood to the desk as a guide to slide the paper against.

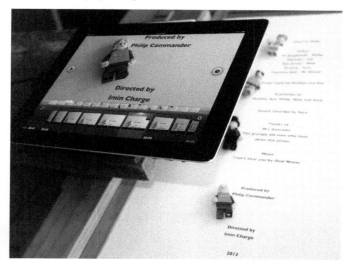

Smooth scrolling requires even movements between pictures. Use time lapse with a two second interval. After each picture use the onscreen overlay as a guide to move the sheet upwards a specific distance such as the height of one line of text.

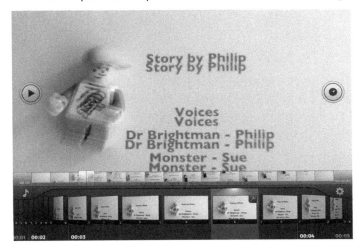

With a longer time lapse interval the LEGO characters could be animated and interact with the text as the credits scroll.

Scrolling credits could also be recorded as video, but iStopMotion allows much greater control over picture exposure, white balance, focus and animation effects.

Photos or real people

If your stop motion is a team project, it can be a good idea to show a picture of each person instead of just their name. This can be done using real people or cut out photos.

Use the overlay to guide each person to sit with their eyes in the same position.

Stand behind the iPad camera to encourage the person to look in the right direction. Record each person for one minute using **time lapse with a one second interval**. This should give more pictures than you need for a playback speed up to 30 FPS.

273

Titles in iMovie

iMovie has a small range of built-in styles for adding text into movies. iMovie titles are:

- Quick and easy to use
- Professional designs with animations.

Stardard iMovie titles

The biggest drawback with iMovie titles is they are designed for a small number of words (around six). Breaking a text into several screens can work, but in most cases the animations (to reveal and hide each title) dominate.

Customising iMovie titles

When you have several screens of titles, create a more compact title sequence with this two step method:

- Create an iMovie project with each block of text on a five second clip
- Save the movie to Camera Roll
- Open a new iMovie project
- Import the first movie
- Split the video to trim the animation off each clip leaving just the titles.

Scrolling credits

Scrolling credits can be recorded as video. The result is very smooth, but iMovie doesn't offer as much control over picture exposure, white balance and focus as iStopMotion.

Thanks for taking this animation journey with us

In this book, you've looked at many ways to create the story or script for your stop motion, including improvisation with the use of story outline questions.

You recorded the soundtrack in GarageBand, with clear processes to record dramatic voices and then edit them, along with sound effects and music, into a rich soundtrack.

You created sets with characters and backgrounds, and recorded animation pictures to match the soundtrack and show the story.

You added a title and credits.

You're an animator:)

One of our main goals in this book is to help you make clear decisions by following procedures which almost guarantee that even your first iPad Animation will be successful.

Happy animating,

Craig Lauridsen

CPSIA information can be obtained
at www.ICGtesting.com
Printed in the USA
BVHW02s1521241018
531112BV00017B/284/P